Hard-Core Truths
about Betrayed Spouses,
Prodigals, and Their Paramours

Hard-Core Truths about Betrayed Spouses, Prodigals, and Their Paramours

Peeling Back the Layers

Dr. Ann Eneh

To the many betrayed spouses whose marriages have been rocked by adultery, I want you to know you're not alone. Stand strong and be encouraged because patience is a weapon that forces deceit to reveal itself.

Contents

Acknowledgments

I am forever grateful to God Almighty, who showed up in the midst of my devastation and transformed my life for the better. Thank You, God, for helping me understand that I didn't have to earn Your love. Thank You for guiding and directing my steps in this difficult time. My wish is for other betrayed spouses, prodigals, and paramours to come to know You. People never remain the same once they encounter Jesus.

My sincere appreciation is expressed to my brilliant young daughter, Emma. She has truly been an inspiration throughout this entire process, always praying and encouraging me to finish what I started. Here's to you, Emma. I acknowledge our furry friends Mohawk and Rio, whose tails never stop wagging and stayed clear as if they knew Mom didn't want to be disturbed during busy times at the computer keyboard. My heartfelt gratitude goes to my parents, Mr. and Mrs. Robert Ojeah (deceased), who taught me early on to trust in God and never to give up on Him or family no matter what. Thank you for instilling those virtues in me.

I'm humbled by the many stories I've read on numerous platforms about resilience in coping with betrayal. Sometimes shared suffering pushes mere strangers together. They build each other up because they believe that they crossed paths for a reason. Betrayal from adultery devastates families, and healing from that pain can take a lifetime. I want betrayed spouses to know that they're not alone. God is with you every step of the way. You just have to reach out and ask Him for help.

Introduction

Adultery is not a new concept in human history. Many cultures consider this to be a very serious crime. God abhors adultery as shown in the Bible. It was the seventh of the Ten Commandments given to Moses by God: "You shall not commit adultery" (Exodus 20:14). Marriage is a sacred institution. It is clearly laid out in the Bible for all to see: "Let marriage be held in honor among all, and let the marriage bed be undefiled; for God will judge the immoral and adulterous" (Hebrews 13:4). When prodigal spouses commit adultery, it goes against their other marriage vows, and the wound inflicted strikes at the core of the betrayed spouses lives. The collateral damage done extends far beyond the couple and their children, spilling over to the next generation.

Thousands of marriages are rocked every year by adultery. I am certain that many couples today are fishing for answers to what went wrong in their seemingly happy marriages. This book is an attempt to answer some questions from a Christian perspective. The truth is not always easy to hear, especially when it exposes certain aspects of our lives we'd rather keep hidden. Jesus told us that the truth will set us free. It is not to be assumed that peeling back layers in the lives of betrayed spouses, prodigals, and their paramours makes them bad people. Neither is it an attempt to shame or guilt-trip them into repentance. Rather, we seek to understand why this is happening and how you, as someone who loves them, can contribute to effect change.

My hope is that this book finds you in your place of need and that you have an open mind to go through each chapter with a fine-tooth comb before making any conclusions. Not everyone is expected to agree with the author and that is quite okay. If this book brings about a change in one prodigal spouse and helps to reconcile one family, then my work here is done.

The contents of this book stem from my own experiences as a betrayed spouse, with the self-help books and resources used, and my belief in God as a Catholic Christian. Betrayed spouses in violent and abusive relationships should get out and seek help to protect themselves and their children. You can love your prodigal from afar when standing for your marriage.

One

And Then It Begins

One of the loneliest places for betrayed spouses to be is living with husbands or wives who have intentionally detached themselves emotionally from you. It is a conscious decision prodigals make to feel less guilty about their cruelty toward their spouses. I don't exactly know what goes on in people's minds, but once this happens you begin noticing subtle changes in your husband or wife. Initially you might simply just ignore it. However, as time passes you cannot help acknowledging that something isn't quite right.

Your spouse might appear moody on certain days, maybe angry, critical of you, or quite rude. They might be happy one day with a surprise gift for you (mostly to ease their guilt), and the next day rain down burning coals on your head. You're left feeling perplexed and asking, "What's going on?" That's okay! I've found myself asking this too. Just know that a prodigal spouse's actions are more destructive than a tornado in June, and their ways are sneakier than a snake in the garden of Eden. As bad as that sounds, 1 Corinthians 10:13 reminds us, "No temptation has overtaken you that is not common to man. God is faithful, and he will not let you be tempted beyond your strength, but with the temptation will also provide the way of escape, that you may be able to endure it." Whew! Therein lies our hope for the future as we waddle through this treacherous terrain. May God's words comfort us and provide soothing balm for our souls. Amen!

Before I delve any further into this topic, I'd like you to know that your prodigal's lack of remorse does not in any way, shape, or form devalue your pain and suffering as a betrayed spouse. Someone once said, "Betrayal is not measured by the act; it is measured by the pain it causes the person being hurt." The spouse's lack of empathy toward you is more of a reflection of them as a person than of you—the betrayed spouse. The Bible tells us that "A man without self-control is like a city broken into and left without walls" (Proverbs 25:28). A prodigal's behavior is all so confusing. Believe me—I know. I get it because I've been there. You find yourself wondering if your husband or wife is now possessed by a demon. They become so mean and are generally not moved by your emotions and would walk right past you even if you were crying a bucketload of tears. Why would the spouse really care? To them, you've become quite an inconvenience, a nagging, annoying, and miserable partner they'd rather not be around. Once a prodigal is involved in an affair, their feelings toward you change. It's not rocket science. You just know it. You feel it in your gut, and that feeling is almost always right.

A prodigal spouse's mind switches gears to the "ignore and deflect mode." They gaslight, stonewall, and manipulate you into thinking you've lost your marbles. If you're not careful, your spouse's truth about the situation soon becomes your truth. Once your relationship with your spouse reaches this point, the freedom of speech in your home loses its filter. Your prodigal spouse now opens the floodgates of criticism, meanness, and rejection to a whole other level.

What's a person to do? Retaliate? Or as some Christians would say, "Put on the whole amor of God" (Ephesians 6:11). Believe me—I think most of us would rather do the former than the later since we are frustrated out of our minds. Do you really deserve that kind of behavior from a spouse who has just betrayed you? Absolutely not! You deserve way better than that, and yet you find yourself sinking deeper into a rabbit hole every time you encounter your double-minded spouse. Unfortunately for you, that endless rabbit hole has no immediate exit passages just yet.

You see, trying to negotiate with a prodigal is like pushing water uphill. Don't do it. It's a trap to get you to lose your cool. Once that happens, it gives them the incentive needed to justify their actions. Don't worry if you've fallen into that trap. I, too, have taken the bait a couple times. Needless to say, it did not end well. I fell right into the slippery slope of "gotcha" and it took forever to climb my way back up. Don't be like me.

At times loving another means limiting our own freedoms. Their unpredictable actions back you into a corner that sets off alarm bells for fight or flight. Regardless of what is happening around you, you must not forget what you know to be true about God. As a praying betrayed spouse, you know that when God's

Word and God's Spirit work together, that same power that formed the universe resides within you. Though your enemies may sit on the throne, you rule them by prayer because godliness is more powerful than anything. As J. R. R. Tolkien eloquently put it at the end of *The Lord of the Rings,* "No one likes tough times, but those tests add power to our testimony."

At other times the betrayed spouse may be tempted to turn the tide on the prodigal and tell them who's boss. But I have to tell you—it's best to regroup or you'll find yourself playing an endless game of Whac-A-Mole. You get exhausted very quickly. My advice? Conserve that energy—because you'll need it to fight the spiritual battle that's about to unfold.

Two

Prodigal Spouses

H. Norman Wright's definition of a prodigal in his book Loving a Prodigal adequately captures its true meaning:

A prodigal is someone who goes against the family's value system. A prodigal says, "I'd rather go this way, and I choose to reject all this over here." In a sense, it's going counter-culture to the way the person has been raised. Prodigals have an intensity in their rebellion that is missing in the actions of other highly disobedient kids.

Now tie that into the meaning of a prodigal spouse.

Who Is a Prodigal Spouse?

For the purposes of this book, *a prodigal spouse is a husband or wife who walks away from their marriage and family to pursue their own interests.* Prodigal spouses devastate family members by leaving a deep wedge of brokenness and scarring in the lives of those who love them. The characters they present are quite peculiar. Dave Harvey accurately describes them in his book *Letting Go: Rugged Love for Wayward*

Souls as "lack of personal responsibility, victim mentality, assertion of rights and independence, and manipulative threat of flight" (p. 43).

In my candid opinion, I think that most prodigal spouses love the convenience of marriage but don't value the institution of marriage. That is why even when involved in illicit affairs, many of them seek to maintain the support they get from family members and the familiarity the marriage provides. They want to eat their cake and have it too. Dr. Joe Beam of MarriageHelper.com writes, "You do not throw away what you have unless you know what you are going to will be better." This obviously further reinforces the point made earlier on.

Prodigal spouses are selfish bullies. They demean their spouses and threaten to leave them all the time (it's part of their mode of operation). These individuals are insecure and project their insecurities onto their spouses. They may have suffered some kind of unresolved childhood trauma or other traumatic life events before they ever met you. So don't go blaming yourself when your prodigal begins acting out after marriage. My father once told me, "A man's true character exudes during stressful life situations." Now I can truly say that I agree with him. Goose bumps? That's my father's way of telling me he heard that. Thank you, Dad.

In any case, when your prodigal acts out, focus instead on how to help them identify any emotional trauma they may have suffered during childhood. Then encourage them to get help. They'd likely resist at first, but when it's done out of love without any expectations, you just might succeed in convincing them to do so. It's referenced in the Bible in Proverbs 15:1—"A soft answer turns away wrath, but a harsh word stirs up anger." So go easy on your prodigal spouse. If you truly love them, then you must learn the three P's:

- Pray for the prodigal—because prayer changes things.
- Persist in prayer—because it's powerfully effective.
- Provide support as necessary and as allowed by the prodigal for healing to begin.

Prodigals have to confront their demons. There's no running away from them. Remember that *hurt people hurt people.* Your prodigal is hurt and most likely will hurt you too, including possible acts of violence or abuse. When that happens, please get out and seek help and support for your safety and for your children. The prodigal will tell a lot of lies to cover up their tracks and play victim for whoever falls for their sob story. Be warned about this, because a person fleeing God is not a reliable witness to God's truth. Therefore, exercise caution when passing judgment on the betrayed spouse since you've been privy to only one version of the story. The betrayed spouse who is already suffering from devastation also gets weighted down with a double vest of shame. They don't need additional daggers flying in their direction. The Bible tells us in Proverbs 19:9 that "A false witness will not go unpunished, and he who utters lies will perish." It is customary to hear from both parties in a dispute before any conclusions are drawn. Ask God to help reveal what the truth really is. Martin Luther said, "The recognition of sin is the beginning of salvation."

A prodigal spouse's life is shrouded in secrecy. For such a person, showing vulnerability is a big step since the prodigal spouse fears their spouse's criticism and judgment. As a result, couples must learn to show their rough edges without fear of rejection from their spouses. No one is perfect, so quit trying to breathe under water. You're not a fish and you don't have gills. Couples should instead take steps to expose their true selves to each other and share without inhibition. This can be done through simple and honest communication. However, the prodigal spouses who cheat have found a way to expose their vulnerabilities to the wrong people—the paramours (illicit sexual partners of married persons) who do not judge or criticize them. This is how affairs start, when they begin sharing intimate details about themselves with the opposite sex. In time, this builds emotional connection and blossoms into a sordid affair that spells trouble for those involved.

It is always safer for spouses to be open and honest about their feelings for each other and let the chips fall where they may. People should be courageous enough to take life's lumps and rejections, don't you think? After all, marriage is not a bed of roses. Even roses themselves have thorns. But the funny thing here is that your so-called "macho man" or "ladybug bear" fears your criticisms, judgments, and rejections if they show you who they are. In order for couples to feel safe enough to share their deepest, darkest secrets with each other, they ought to have created a safe-enough environment, devoid of preconceived notions, right off the bat. That is not to say that these connections cannot be built and worked on over time. Surely we all have skeletons in our closets, right?—though some with varying degrees of what could be revealed if we ever went looking.

There truly can be no secrets if you ever want your marriage to work. Secrets always divide and it's a hunting game with you as prey. The Bible warns us in 1 Peter 5:8, "Be sober, be watchful. Your adversary the devil prowls around like a roaring lion, seeking someone to devour." You don't want to know what would happen if you dressed up like a lamb in front of a hungry lion. Don't give Satan any wiggle room in your marriage or he'll take home and destroy it. William P. Young said, "We are as sick as the secrets we keep. The only way out is to go right through it. When secrets are exposed, they lose their power over you." I totally agree with him. Though prodigal spouses don't want their secret affairs uncovered, most would ultimately feel great relief when they become known and the pressure they've carried for so long is released. It's almost like a patient with pneumothorax who finds it difficult to breathe as a result of air being trapped in the chest cavity. Can you imagine the relief they feel when that trapped air is suddenly released by the insertion of a chest tube? Now you get the idea.

A little throwback here: Do you remember the woman caught in the act of adultery in the Bible? Those accusers, or "brood of vipers" as I'd love to call them (to borrow John the Baptist's and Jesus's expression), wanted to stone her to death—you know, those holier-than-thou ones. Let's see if you've read your Bible. What was Jesus's reply to them when they asked Him what they were to do with her? Let me remind you where you can find that story in the Bible: John 8:3–11. I just love what Jesus told them:

"Let him who is without sin among you be the first to throw a stone at her" (v. 7).

How many people do you think stoned her? None! The Bible says in Romans 3:23, "All have sinned and fall short of the glory of God." I know what you're thinking, but I in no way condone adultery in marriage, and I certainly do not minimize the pain and devastation a betrayed spouse feels. Not even close! All I'm saying is that we should examine ourselves first before throwing shade at others, and then work toward reconciliation if possible. God hates divorce. I'll keep reminding us throughout this book until it sinks in.

Marriage was not designed for divorce right from the beginning. It was the sinfulness of man that allowed it. I understand if your prodigal refuses help initially because of guilt, pride, and shame. But with your persistence and unconditional love, you just might win them over so that a breakthrough happens. Good always trumps evil.

Inasmuch as this is true, you must also acknowledge that not all marriages are restored. As they say, "Not everything that's broken is meant to be fixed." In that case, God, who designed marriage, has bigger plans for you. Wait on Him to rain down that particular blessing meant just for you. Jeremiah 29:11 says, "I know the plans I have for you, says the Lord, plans for welfare and not for evil, to give you a future and a hope." Amen!

Because of my own experience as a betrayed spouse, I think it's easier for a woman to be vulnerable with her man than for a man to be vulnerable with his woman. Following betrayal, we all want to move forward in our relationships since no one wants to remain stuck or be held permanently in limbo. However, some of us in these moments don't know what to do or which way to turn. We need a little help and a sense of direction when numbed by this tragedy. According to C. S. Lewis, "We all want progress, but if you're on the wrong road, progress means doing an about-turn and walking back to the right road; in that case, the man who turns back soonest is the most progressive." I don't know about you, but here are some of the things I've heard from the grapevine regarding men:

- All men cheat.
- It's a man's world out there.
- No matter how good a woman is, her husband will always cheat on her.
- Men are born to spread their seed.

The list goes on and on and on. Let me know if I missed anything. Though some might argue that there's some truth to these claims, others just call them plain crazy talk. I don't believe that to be true. I think it's a matter of choice. It depends on the individual and what risks they're willing to take to satisfy their carnal urges. It also depends on the person's belief and value systems. But then again, prodigals have no moral compass. Their beliefs and values went out the door the minute they aligned themselves with the devil, who in turn made them puppets in his ploy to destroy not only every family but also every church and society itself. In such instances, the prodigals witfully becomes the devil's advocate to carry out his will.

For us humans, the choices we make changes who we become. The prodigal spouse sees sin as attractive because of the candy coating it usually presents. They jump in headfirst and absquatulates before anyone can say, "Jack Robinson." Their families are left behind to suffer the devastating consequences of their actions. People tell me that men are mostly drawn to what they can't have, so keep that in mind, ladies. I also read that most men will leave a woman for another woman who will tolerate their lies. However, Tiktokers seem to think that a woman who genuinely loves her man leaves him only for herself. She would have given him chance after chance to make things right, but in the end something has to give. You don't have to believe my word for it—just ask Tiktokers. If we can't seem to adjudicate on the matter, then I'd vote for us to adjourn until next time.

Whatever Which Way: We Need Answers

Have you reached a point in your marriage at which you're conflicted as to whether to stay in what's left of it or to go? You remember your wedding vows if you're a Christian and shudder to think how this could have happened. Your world came crashing down in one fell swoop, much without warning. Actually, there were warning signs—you simply ignored them. These things don't just happen overnight. After all, Rome was not built in a day. If you're being completely honest with yourself, you would remember some red flags you probably shouldn't have ignored.

I know you may think about what the dreams for your marriage could have been before it took a dramatic hairpin turn. Every day you go over that scenario a million times in your head until it turns into a dizzying spell. Fear not—you're not alone. I find myself replaying same old tunes until they get pretty stuck in my head. For what it's worth, SpongeBob hated that too.

When it comes to wedding vows these days, do they mean anything anymore to anyone? Why is it so easy for a man and woman to break their commitment and not feel as though they've done something wrong? Why is it always the betrayed spouse's fault? The cheating spouse almost always blames the faithful spouse. What is so fundamentally broken in a man or woman's life that makes them act this way? What causes these unacceptable behaviors to resurface later on in life? Were there warning signs when you were dating that you perhaps ignored? Were they so good at hiding red flags that you never really noticed them until now? Is it that prodigal spouses have gotten so good at keeping the lid on so no one is aware that they lead a double life? Why are prodigal spouses so good to others but never to their betrayed spouses? Why are they so terrified of being found out? Better yet, why do unfaithful spouses disparage their betrayed spouses to others? Why do most prodigals follow the exact same pattern of blame, deflecting and rejecting? Is this midlife crisis or unresolved childhood trauma now bursting out of its seams? Has the medical society failed to adequately address midlife crisis in certain age groups? Why does our society accept irreconcilable differences as part of reasons for divorce? Should these types of behaviors (adultery and abandonment) not carry hefty penalties in the court of law?

I rack my brain for answers to find which way is up. Someone said to me a long time ago, "When you let something simmer too long, it will boil over and extinguish your pilot light." Is this what is happening to our prodigal spouses? I think that as betrayed spouses, we must come together and take a stand—for what we tolerate, we fertilize. Some educational resources on marriage tell us to set up boundaries and follow the "Love must be tough" rule. Other religious books tell women to love unconditionally and emulate the life of the virtuous woman described in the Bible. Really! I see their lips moving but can't quite seem to hear what they're saying. Don't they get it? Your life has just imploded, and as in slow motion, you're watching yourself in free fall. And you say what now? That's the best you have? Is this really what you to hear this very moment?

Look—it's okay if you can't make any decisions just yet because you're still too raw, too numb, and too terrified to make sense of what's happening. So stop already! Just take a step back. Give people time to think before you bombard them with your opinions. This is all too much and you're not helping by this information overload. I imagine all you want to do right now is crawl into bed and wish it all away. Maybe if you shut your eyes and cock your ears long enough, you'll realize it was only just a bad dream. No, this is no "abracadabra." It's as real as it gets, so get ready for the rough ride. They say that sometimes in life you have to experience the bad to appreciate the good.

Readers: If you have answers to any of these questions, please let us know on our YouTube website, "Hope for the Betrayed," at tiny.cc/ctotnz. Throughout this book I'll frequently post our site's link as a reminder to let your voices be heard. Let us engage in meaningful conversation about issues dearest to our hearts and work together as a community to address them.

The Prodigal Spouse's Rebellion

Sometimes in their season of rebellion, prodigals will increase in misery to a point at which they would not be able to live with themselves. Hallelujah! As someone once said, "Reality has a way of shattering fantasies, no matter how long they've survived or how deeply love is felt." Keep in mind that adulterous relationships are borne out of lies and most definitely will end in misery. Now, how many of you shouted from your lips to God's ears? For the record, I did too. Benjamin Franklin said, "Guests, like fish, begin to smell after three days." If your prodigal has moved out and is currently living with the other person, I bet you wish that were true. A prodigal's affair with the other person can be likened to a rotten seed that bears no good fruit. It eventually withers much like the fig tree in the Bible after Jesus cursed it.

Then why can't prodigals see it for what it is, that nothing good will come of an adulterous affair? You tell me! According to Albert Einstein, "No problems can be solved by the same consciousness that created it." That's no wonder, considering that prodigals are spiritually blinded by their sins and are unstable, to say the least. They are temporarily out of commission and are often sucked into the abyss of an "affair fog" (an illusion not grounded in reality). This is fool's gold they are digging. You'd think! They must not have gotten the memo the rest of us did—the one that says, "Not all that glitters is gold."

These words from Levi Lusko hit home for me: "After going through the candy coating, all sin has to offer is heartbreak, bitterness, and regret." No matter how far we've fallen, nothing can separate us from the love of God. I couldn't have said it any better myself. Have you ever sensed that when your prodigal is in trouble, the first person they think to reach out to is you, the betrayed spouse? Why is that? It's because the paramour does not have the deep roots needed to carry that burden and tends to flee the scene when the relationship is no longer beneficial. It is mind-boggling when prodigals move from one adulterous affair to another. You can't keep performing the same actions and expect a different result, right? Maybe someone ought to tell them to watch the *Looney Tunes* cartoons. Better yet, I'd recommend watching *Tom and Jerry*. Here they'd hopefully grasp the concept that performing the same actions over and over again will not result in a different outcome. Ever wish this analogy might ring through to them? Yeah! Me too. You see, prodigals are like addicts, and addicts cannot just go cold turkey.

Also, "people in emotionally charged affairs have trouble ending it." So there's that.

Inside the Mind of a Prodigal Spouse

A statement worth mentioning by C. S. Lewis in line with this book goes like this:

> Every time you make a choice you are turning the central part of you, the part of you that chooses, into something a little different from what it was before. And taking your life as a whole, with all your innumerable choices, all your life long you are slowly turning this central thing into a heavenly creature or into a hellish creature: either into a creature that is in harmony with God, and with other creatures, and with itself, or else into one that is in a state of war and hatred with God, and with its fellow-creatures, and with itself. . . . Each of us at each moment is progressing to one state or the other.

Have you noticed that prodigal spouses waffle back and forth? They are indecisive and so conflicted. One minute they can be loving toward their spouses and the next they are as cold as ice. The tempo changes very quickly. You want to know why? Simple—just look in your Bible:

> "You are of your father the devil, and your will is to do your father's desires. He was a murderer from the beginning,

and has nothing to do with the truth, because there is no truth in him. When he lies, he speaks according to his own nature, for he is a liar and the father of lies." (John 8:44)

You can now fully understand that your prodigal spouse has been taken captive by the devil to do his bidding. This may very well answer the question betrayed spouses have been asking about their prodigals for decades. I, too, have asked exactly the same questions. It is not at all uncommon to read comments from betrayed spouses on marriage blogs and elsewhere stating, "This isn't who I married," "They're acting very strangely," "It's like someone else has taken over them," "They've gone crazy all of a sudden," or "I think my husband or wife is possessed." The list goes on and on. Inasmuch as this has happened to your prodigal, they, too, were complacent in allowing themselves to be used as the devil's pawn. The Bible tells us to resist the devil and he'll flee from us. James 4:7 commands us, "Submit yourselves therefore to God. Resist the devil and he will flee from you." Nevertheless, our prodigals need our intercessory prayers for God to set them free from Satan's grip. Remember that "God is not a God of confusion but of peace" (1 Corinthians 14:33).

Prayer: *Father God, I pray that You cover us with the blood of Jesus. I decree and declare that our husbands [wives] are set free right now in the powerful name of Jesus. Amen! I release them from the shackles and chains of bondage in the mighty name of Jesus. Amen! Father God, I stand on 1 Samuel 10:6, which says, "Then the Spirit* *of the Lord will come mightily upon you, and you shall prophesy with them and be turned into another man." Amen!*

Remember physics class way back in high school? That subject was clearly not my forte. However, one thing that stood out for me was learning about Newton's first law of motion, which states that once an object is in motion, it will keep moving unless it is acted upon by another force. Now imagine the mind of a prodigal constantly plagued by false beliefs created in their minds. Does this set off alarm bells yet? Their reality becomes rooted in these false beliefs. Now what do you think would happen? The prodigal off course would act on them on a daily basis until something else takes over. How would this come about? Yes! You guessed right—in a word, *prayer!* That's why it's so important that you pray for the prodigal. It's only through your prayers that these false beliefs are altered and replaced by the Word of God, penetrating the prodigal's hardened heart and thus renewing their minds. This process creates a renewed sense of hope and direction in the prodigal's life. Hardened hearts are transformed by God through godly repentance. The Bible confirms this in 2 Corinthians 7:10: "For godly grief produces a repentance that leads to salvation and brings no regret, but worldly grief produces death. " Jesus reminds us, "There is joy before the angels of God over one sinner who repents" (Luke 15:10).

To buttress the point made earlier, let's look at this from another perspective. The prodigal spouse goes through a period of what we can call a "metamorphosis" (change), much like a butterfly. It starts off ugly, as a caterpillar, whose appetite is ferocious. With time it becomes encased in a chrysalis (pupa stage), where it stays silent until ready. The pupa eventually morphs into a beautiful butterfly that is ready to take its first flight.

Conversely, the prodigal spouse starts off ugly—abandoning a moral code of values, family, and friends to take on guilt, shame, and self-condemnation (ugly caterpillar stage). They go silent and break contact with family and friends for a while (pupa stage) until ready to break free of sin. Through your intercessory prayer and fasting, the prodigal sheds their cloak of shame, guilt, and self-condemnation just in time to take on a new identity in Christ as a new creation. Romans 12:2 encourages us, "Do not be conformed to this world but be transformed by the renewal of your mind, that you may prove what is the will of God, what is good and acceptable and perfect."

Let's be clear: it is only God who can change our minds. For prodigal spouses who have abandoned their morals and values, only God's divine intervention can help them conquer their demons. The Bible tells us that we should delight ourselves in the Lord and He'll give us the desires of our hearts. We desire our prodigals to find their way back to God. Again, we must remember that the choices we make change who we become. Repeat this to yourself until it becomes part of you.

Another thing worth mentioning here is that when a prodigal spouse voices the need for "space" to think things through, in my candid opinion that is simply nonsense. The prodigal has already made up their mind and is simply just looking for a way out. Prodigals want to use this so-called "space" to be with their paramour if they are already involved in an illicit affair. That way, they no longer have to worry or make up stories about their whereabouts when asked by their significant other. While some might actually use this time to reflect on what their life would look like as a single person again, others might simply want to confirm for themselves if the grass is truly greener on the other side. You know—"try it on for size."

But here's the downside to this acquired new freedom—they proceed with the same baggage to whatever new relationships they are in. Guess what—since these problems don't automatically disappear with the paramour, that same pattern repeats itself, often turning into a vicious cycle with detrimental outcomes.

The paramour might be willing to put up with the fiasco at first, because they fear losing out to you (the wife or husband). So sad really! The paramour thinks it's a competition between you two, but in reality they weren't even in the game. Just like the prodigal, the paramour is also living a lie. They'd continue to tolerate your prodigal's behavior because of the financial gains involved. But in the long run, they'd also walk and bail on the prodigal when the relationship no longer serves its purpose. As stated earlier, the prodigal spouse constantly lies and is blind to the truth. It is therefore incumbent on you as the one who loves them to pray for God to remove the spiritual blinders so the truth can be revealed. Dr. Tony Evans put it ever so eloquently: "Satan cannot thrive in the atmosphere of God's truth."

Prayer: *Father God, I pray that You remove spiritual blinders for prodigal spouses to see the truth, for the truth shall surely set them free. I pray that You remove all negative influences from their lives, especially those that offer ungodly counsel. Help us to love one another as You have loved us. Amen!*

Married Life 101

It is our responsibility as husbands and wives to provide a safe and nurturing environment for our spouses to air their grievances without judgment or criticism. Easier said than done? I hear you! Many times I, too, forgot to zip my lips and stirred up a dormant volcano. That aside, we have to try to work things out without shaming them. This goes both ways for either spouse. I think that as married couples, we must never stop investing in our relationships. The moment we do, we begin taking things for granted.

This steady decline may not become immediately apparent, but as time passes you find that things are no longer what they used to be. Don't get me wrong—this does not give the prodigal a free pass to act out in unacceptable ways or is meant to invalidate the betrayed spouse's pain. This reminder only calls your attention to the bigger picture and then taking steps toward healing and marriage reconciliation.

Remember also that prodigal spouses have egos as big as Mount Everest. Their pride is so big that their ignorance can't fight it. It's not at all surprising that they make such lousy decisions that make no sense to us. Nevertheless, there's hope since we know that the chicken comes home to roost. But before sanity boomerangs back home, the damage would have been done and the trail of carnage left behind would have extended far longer than the Mississippi River.

As people who love our prodigals, we must pray without ceasing as the Bible commands us to do in 1 Thessalonians 5:17. Prodigals have no justification for bailing on their families even when they claim to be in unhealthy marriages (except for abuse and violence). They could have followed the proper channels and filed for divorce or gone to counseling if they so wished. They didn't have to cheat—period. So pay no attention to all the background noise because there's absolutely no justification for cheating.

Illegitimate children are conceived through adultery when impatience marries unbelief. How do you explain to your born-out-of-wedlock child how they came to be? Do you really think your Ishmael wants to be referred to as a "love child"? I think not. You and your indiscretions have probably set this child up for failure considering the circumstances surrounding how they were conceived. Listen up, prodigals—if you can't take the heat, then get out of the kitchen. The residue of sin is always hard. No amount of detergent or bleach can wash it clean unless it is washed in the blood of the lamb. Amen! The Bible says in Isaiah 1:18, "Come now, let us reason together, says the Lord: though your sins are like scarlet, they shall be as white as snow; though they are red like crimson, they shall become like wool." As a prodigal spouse, you must be willing to admit and confess your sins in order to be saved.

Job 4:7–9 says, "Think now, who that was innocent ever perished? Or where were the upright cut off? As I have seen, those who plow iniquity and sow trouble reap the same. By the breath of God they perish, and by the blast of his anger they are consumed." Amen!

Sometimes in life the messes we create overwhelm us. In a bid to wiggle out of them, we end up piling them up instead. But take courage! Don't lose faith, for where there's life, there's hope. Tragedy often makes us stronger. I encourage betrayed spouses to leave their prodigals to God, "for the Lord disciplines him whom he loves, and chastises every son whom he receives" (Hebrews 12:6). He'll get their attention one way or the other when the time is right. Your job is to pray without ceasing and never, ever give up. James 5:16 tells us that "The prayer of a righteous man has great power in its effects."

Question: What would you say to discourage a man from cheating on his wife or a woman from cheating on her husband? Go to tiny.cc/ctotnz to voice your opinion.

What the Prodigal with Multiple Paramours Should Know

For the rebellious prodigal spouse with multiple sexual partners, do you really want to be referred to as a doorknob where everybody gets a turn? I certainly hope not, because you are created in the image of God. He is here with open arms to accept you as His child just as you are. You need only to confess your sins and declare that Jesus Christ is Lord.

Don't you think for a second that you are too damaged or too far gone to be saved. Jesus was born for people such as these. The Bible tells us in 1 John 1:9, "If we confess our sins, he is faithful and just, and will forgive our sins and cleanse us from all unrighteousness." It doesn't get any better than that. When we get a 10- or 15-percent discount coupon, we go crazy and rush to the store to take advantage of that promotion. Hello! Jesus is giving you a 110-percent discount for your sins. You'd be crazy not to take it. He's giving you a way out even when you don't deserve it. Take it and run with it, my friend. Use this opportunity so graciously offered to redeem your soul from total condemnation.

Don't let anything or anyone stop you. Check your shame and guilt at the door and don't take them back up. Tell them they are no longer welcome in your life, for you are now in your Father's house. Amen! If you have ears, listen! Acts 2:38 says, "Repent, and be baptized every one of you in the name of Jesus Christ for the forgiveness of your sins; and you shall receive the gift of the Holy Spirit."

Prayer: *My prayer for prodigal spouses today is that they take a stand to become followers of Christ. May they never shrink back and be destroyed by the pleasures this world offers them (Hebrews 10:39). I pray that God uses this tragedy to turn our prodigals into His disciples and for Christ to make them fishers of men. Amen!*

I encourage all prodigals to visit marriage blogs, message boards, prayer walls online or in person, watch YouTube videos on marriage testimonials to see the havoc created when you walked out and left your families behind. What are you waiting for? Go see for yourselves the effects of adultery and abandonment on families. Put a bookmarker on and return after you've completed this assignment. It's not a pretty picture. Remember Proverbs 11:21: "Be assured, an evil man will not go unpunished, but those who are righteous will be delivered."

Prayer: *I pray that completing this exercise will lead to a softening of all prodigals' hardened hearts in the name of Jesus. Amen! I pray that they'll be prompted by the Holy Spirit to open up lines of communication with their spouses and set a course for home. Amen!*

Let the Truth Be Told

For the prodigal husband or wife, if you know deep down in your heart and soul that you'd rather not work on restoring your marriage, then for heaven's sake, don't just disappear without a trace. Stop tying your spouse down for selfish reasons. Man up or woman up, set your spouses free, and send them a way out. This is because some will never walk away. Don't wait, five, ten, twenty, or even thirty years to return all used up for your betrayed spouse to take care of you in your old age. That wouldn't be fair.

You see, I think prodigal spouses are running away from God and from their spouses. It's easier for the prodigal spouse to disappear, hence the silence no matter how much their betrayed spouses try to initiate communication. It's also true that when people know that they have wronged someone, they tend to avoid that person at all costs to ease their guilt and shame. If you've ever wondered why prodigals choose not to communicate with their spouses at all, here are five possible reasons:

- The prodigals' paramour may have forbidden them from contacting their spouses in any way, shape, or form.
- The prodigals do not want their spouses to change their minds about the marriage.
- The prodigals want to uncouple and therefore want their spouses to move on with life without them.
- It's far less painful and easier for the prodigals to ignore their spouses than to talk to them.
- The prodigals do not want their spouses to pressure them into coming back to the marriage.

A man or woman who knows you're married and engages in sexual relationship with you does not love you. Do I have to say this again? Here goes! *A man or woman who knows you're married and engages in sexual relationship with you does not love you.* Prodigals, hear me and get this message through your thick skulls—this isn't love but rather a fiery and seductive one-way ticket to hell. Remember: "The wages of sin is death" (Romans 3:23). If you think for a moment that you and your paramour will someday ride off into the sunset and live happily ever after, then you might as well put the "I'm stupid" hat on your head.

Beware the Company You Keep

For the prodigal who makes it a habit of not coming home for family dinners and makes up excuses about "working late," remember that your children are watching and could well model your type of behavior in the future. Spend time with your family today because tomorrow is never guaranteed. As a married man or woman, you have no business creating dating profiles on dating apps. You are already taken, in case you had forgotten. The question is—What are you doing on a dating site if not asking for trouble? Beware of the company you keep if you have friends who practice such. Their bad behavior will surely rub off on you.

The Bible tells us in Proverbs 27:17, "Iron sharpens iron, and one man sharpens another." But don't take my word for it. Just ask Pastor Stephen Furtick, who said, "This is the reason you should stop hanging out with some people. You catch what you're close to." Boom! It's kind of like saying, "Bad company corrupts good morals."

The Bible reminds us in Romans 8:6–8, "To set the mind on the flesh is death, but to set the mind on the spirit is life and peace. For the mind that is set on flesh is hostile to God; it does not submit to God's law, indeed it cannot; and those who are in the flesh cannot please God." In Galatians 5:19–21 we read, "Now the works of the flesh are plain: immorality, impurity, licentiousness, idolatry, sorcery, enmity, strife, jealousy, anger, selfishness, dissension, party spirit, envy, drunkenness, carousing, and the like. I warn you, as I warned you before, that those who do such things shall not inherit the kingdom of God."

The Bible also warns us to not be unequally yoked with unbelievers. I know to err is human, but that's no excuse to indulge in evil deeds. If your husband or wife has a friend who you believe offers them ungodly counsel, pray and talk to them about it. You do not have to associate with that friend or invite them into your home. I hear you saying in that case, "What then should you do?" Good question. You're now caught between your spouse and their ungodly friend. Let us hear what you think at tiny.cc/ctotnz.

Ways the Prodigal Spouse Must Become the Healer

- Stop all contact with the paramour.
- Take responsibility for your actions or inactions.
- Stop being a control freak.
- Be sensitive to your spouse's triggers.
- Show remorse and apologize for the part you played in the demise of your marriage.
- Do away with selfishness and be patient.
- Be truthful and trustworthy.
- Educate yourself about relationships and affairs. Read about the five love languages, his needs, her needs, and so on.
- Stop being so defensive and listen to your spouse.
- Don't blame your spouse for the affair.

- Be loving, supportive, and reassuring.
- Check your anger, guilt, and shame at the door.
- Go to therapy or get some counseling.
- Practice gratitude.
- Avoid secrets and be an open book.
- Attend marriage conferences—together if possible.
- Pray as a family and eat meals together whenever possible.
- Date each other again and ask your spouse daily how you can make their day better.
- Renew your wedding vows.
- Reflect your marital status if you're on social media with photographs of you and your spouse as a couple.
- Wear your wedding band and never take it off.
- Attend church and other functions together.
- Have accountability partners and join in some of your church leadership organizations.
- Be a role model for your children.

Prodigal spouses must commit to not run away or hide when things get difficult. They must continue to be open and willing to dialogue even when preferring not to. This makes all the difference. Moreover, it is only cowardly men and women who run from their problems. The Bible tells us in 2 Timothy 1:7, "For God did not give us a spirit of timidity but a spirit of power and love and self-control."

Author Rayya Elias writes, "The truth has legs; it always stands. When everything else in the room has blown up or dissolved away, the only thing left standing will always be the truth. Since that's where you're going to end up anyway, you might as well just start there."

You must be honest before, during, and after the discovery process. *Drip, drip, drip* just won't cut it. It further delays the healing and recovery process. The prodigal must become an open book in order to gradually build back the broken trust in the relationship. It took some time for your marriage to deteriorate and definitely will take time for it to heal too. Remember: an affair is built upon tension. It is always a good thing to defuse than to add fuel to the fire.

For you ladies, I know that getting a man to talk is sometimes like pulling teeth, so go slowly. If he retreats into his "nothing brain box," let him dwell there for a while and then try again. Our God is so good and will make a way, so don't you dare stop believing in this truth. Restoration will happen in God's own time and if He wills it so.

Things Worth Knowing to Rebuild
Connection with Your Spouse

These add-ons are just little reminders as to why your spouse's love tank might be empty. Just go through them with an open mind:

- Do you pray together and read the Bible as a family?
- Do you know what your spouse thinks and feels about God?
- Do you attend church together as a family?
- Are you both members of a ministry at your church?

- Are you both on the same page when it comes to discipline for your children?
- Do you make time for family?
- Do you address family issues together?
- Do you keep secrets from each other?
- Are you familiar with your spouse's traumatic childhood events?
- Do you resolve conflict, not letting it fester and build resentment over time?
- Do you ask for forgiveness when you do something wrong?
- When was the last time you complimented your spouse?
- When was the last time you bought your spouse a gift "just because"?
- Can you recall the last time you left your spouse a sweet sticky note?
- Do you know your spouse well enough?
- What is your spouse's favorite color?
- What is your spouse's favorite movie or television show?
- What is your spouse's favorite meal?
- Do you know your spouse's sexual fantasies?
- Can you mention your spouse's major aspirations?
- Do you know what your spouse is mostly afraid of?
- When your spouse talks to you, do you put aside your electronic device, listening and making eye contact?
- When was the last time you asked your spouse out on a date or on a weekend getaway?

- Do you come home for family dinners?
- When running late, do you notify your spouse?
- When was the last time you told your spouse that you loved them?
- Do you help around the house?
- Do you respect boundaries you both set?
- Do you know what stresses your spouse currently faces?
- Do you know how your spouse copes with stress?
- Do you avoid telling half-truths or outright lies to your spouse to keep the peace?
- Do you know your spouse's basic philosophy of life?
- Do you love your spouse?
- Do you make time for each other?
- Are you emotionally connected to your spouse?
- Do you refuse to permit in-laws or friends to interfere with your family life?
- When was the last time you had a family vacation?
- Does your wife or husband know if you have a will, insurance policy, or power of attorney?

Prodigal spouses must be honest with themselves and answer these hard-core questions truthfully.

- Do my childhood traumatic events still cause me pain when I think about them?
- Why do I crave validation from other people?

- Do my secrets help me stay in control?
- Am I an addict?
- Did my decision to abandon my family solve my problems?
- How does my behavior affect my family?
- What have I learned about myself as a result of adultery?
- Have I forgiven myself?
- What will freedom from my childhood trauma look like?
- What will freedom from my addiction look like?

Three

The Paramour

A paramour is an illicit sexual partner of a married person. This individual is just as broken as the prodigal and would resort to anything to break up a family for selfish reasons. Paramours take special pride in their notorious reputations as home-wrecker cognoscentes. The prodigal's infatuation with the paramour is like a drug and needs more and more of it to cope with stressful life situations.

I'm not going to get into the full complexities of the human brain functions here. Let's save that for another time. Just know that when prodigals let the paramour go at discovery of the illicit affair, they go through withdrawal. Prodigals who have convinced themselves that they are in love with the paramour are delusional. They think they've found their "soulmates" who understand them. But in reality they've only found someone who can tolerate their delusions for financial gain. Both the prodigal spouse and the paramour live in an alternate universe where the prodigal thinks sex with the paramour is the best thing since sliced bread. They think this way because they have to hide to do it. The thrill that secrecy provides makes the risk worth taking.

Prodigals go into what is known as an "affair fog," which clouds their senses of reasoning. If you've ever wondered why prodigals risk so much for so little, here's your possible answer. This kind of intense love feeling is called "limerence." With time, this intense love feeling fizzles out, leaving them just as empty as they were before.

Paramours are adulterers (third wheels) who know that a man or woman is married and is still willing to engage in a sexual relationship with them. They lack self-respect and probably suffer from very low self-esteem, frequently trading their bodies to fill their loneliness, benefiting from the financial gain the relationship provides. Most of them know that nothing will come of their illicit affairs yet are complicit in helping to devastate families. They, too, like the prodigal, allow themselves to be used as the devil's pawn.

Paramours claim to care deeply for prodigals and for some weird reason believe they're actually "soulmates." They claim that the love they have for your spouse is stronger than an acre of garlic. Give me a break and a barf bag too. Here's the thing: if paramours truly cared for prodigals as they claim, they would not engage in the sins of adultery, knowing full well the consequences they would bring when discovered. If you are to take away one thing from this affair, remember that God will punish adulterers and bring vengeance on them.

Certain paramours may claim not knowing that the prodigal was married. Let's cut the nonsense! Do a basic Google search or pay for a background check. You don't blindly invest in someone in the twenty-first century, knowing the type of world we live in. If the prodigal can lie to you about basic stuff like who they are and their marital status, then what else is the prodigal hiding from you? How would you feel if some other man or woman did that to you? People just don't understand that what goes around comes around. If the affair is ever discovered, prodigals should know that they don't owe the paramour any obligations to remain in the affair. Your loyalty is to your spouse—you know, the person you made your vows to on your wedding day.

I know this sounds a little bit harsh, but getting yourself involved with a married man or woman comes with its own reward. You reap what you sow, and the wages of sin is death. Look in the Bible. Romans 6:23 says, "For the wages of sin is death, but the free gift of God is eternal life in Christ Jesus our Lord." For the record, I'm pretty sure God will not hand over someone else's husband or wife to you on a silver platter. There are many, many singles out there, so go get your own. You may be someone else's prayer request.

Alas! Where were we? I had to get that out of my system. Galatians 6:7 says, "Do not be deceived; God is not mocked, for whatsoever a man sows, that he will also reap." I want you to take the time to ponder these words. Revelation 2:29 says, "He who has an ear, let him hear what the Spirit says to the churches." Inasmuch as paramours deserve what they get, you must also remember that they, too, need healing from whatever experiences life has imprinted on them. Such traumatic life events also cause them to act out and devalue themselves. They somehow believe that they are not good enough and settle in as second best in their illicit relationships.

Hear me! You, too, are God's creation and can be redeemed if you confess your sins and sin no more. Remember the woman at the well in the Bible (John 4:1–26) or the one caught in the act of adultery (John 8:1–11). These stories are great exemplars for you to mull over while waiting for Mr. or Mrs. Right and offer some measures of hope for you if you chose to turn your life around. Just know that the choices you make change who you become.

Most who play the role of paramours have somehow convinced themselves that they do not owe the betrayed spouses any loyalties whatsoever. That may be so, but remember that God will also ask the paramour about the role you played in this love triangle. Marriage consists of two people and not three. As they say, "Two is company and three is a crowd." So beware and know that judgment day is coming for you if you do not repent and walk away. Proverbs 11:22 says, "Like a gold ring in a swine's snout is a beautiful woman without discretion."

A Paramour's Modus Operandi

A paramour's agenda is usually to win over your prodigal's affection through constant praise and affirmation. The paramours seduce the prodigals with their honey-coated tongue to keep the prodigal spellbound. The prodigal who is so drunken with praise disregards the dangers that lurk beneath. They crave the paramour's attention and is insecure about their relationship, knowing how it all started. The prodigal fears that their relationship is doomed to fail only in a matter of time. For this reason, the paramour would go the extra mile to keep things exciting and employs all tactics to keep your prodigal coming in for the kill. The Bible refers to her (as a female) with a description of an adulteress. Proverbs 5:3 says, "For the lips of a loose woman drip honey, and her speech is smoother than oil."

Deep within, the paramours know that what they are doing is wrong, but puts their needs first and finds ways to justify their actions. They abstain from criticizing or judging their illicit lovers no matter what they do. This further draws the lover (prodigal) firmly into the paramour's web of lies. The prodigal spouses disparage their betrayed spouses in front of the paramours to gain their confidence—and the paramours in turn encourages the prodigals. They think they are "soulmates" and wonder how something so wrong could be so right. Hello! This relationship is sinful and was orchestrated from the pit of hell just in case you're wondering. They make you (the betrayed spouse) an outsider and discuss future plans without you.

Some paramours have gotten so insecure and threatened by the prodigals' spouses that they resort to stalking them in person and on social media. As time goes on, they become more demanding of your prodigal's time and affection. They get more and more frustrated with having to be the side-lover and not the actual spouse. They want what you have and will do anything and everything to take your place.

Sometimes prodigals get way over their heads thinking that it's possible to keep their paramours in check but more often than not are deathly mistaken. Paramours call, text, and email your prodigal at odd hours, hoping that you will find out. This tactic, they hope, increases their chances of creating chaos and delivering the death blow that would cripple your marriage. Paramours usually set up a chain of events that separate families without giving it a second thought. They want what they want, and it's your prodigal they want. In their twisted minds, they have concluded that things will serve them better when they become the spouse.

When my husband and I separated, his paramour would text him incessantly whenever he was with me and our daughter. I found that rather amusing. If their so-called "relationship" was so secure, why the epic display of so much insecurity? During those times I held my own, "zipped my lips," and never asked questions until his visit was over. I would then scream into my pillows and cry out to God in prayer. For a while I could have sworn that my phone and computer systems were being hacked. I'm not a hundred-percent sure. But it surely seemed like it back then. Could you imagine your husband or wife being controlled by the third wheel they allowed into their lives, who wasn't supposed to be there? They take orders from the paramour but disregards your gentle nudging to do the right thing. I feel smoke coming out my ears every time I think about this.

In the beginning, when the prodigal and the paramour first began their illicit affair, the paramour would have agreed to remain obscure in their relationship. The paramour was supposed to be only background noise. But as time went on, the paramour became unsatisfied with what was agreed to and longed to upgrade their status. The paramour now wants the prodigal's full attention and proposes marriage. Little Miss Paramour now wants to become Mrs. Prodigal.

The prodigal spouse, however, is unsure of whether to give up their family for the lover. The paramour now ups the ante in hopes for a change and a permanent placement in their life. When this fails, they threaten the prodigal with exposure just as with those before. The minute an affair partner threatens to expose the affair, put them under pressure to leave their family, or resorts to manipulation, should that not set off alarm bells for the prodigal to leave the relationship? I wonder why prodigals still feel obligated to remain. The foolish ones cave under pressure and complies with their paramour's demands.

Some paramours may encourage the prodigal to open other financial accounts in their names or buy new homes, new vehicles, or an assortment of many other items. Some female paramours intentionally become pregnant to trap the prodigal into submission. When this happens, the male prodigal now finds himself at a crossroad, prompting the pendulum to swing. At this juncture he vacillates between you and the paramour and becomes even more agitated and impossible to live with if he is an in-home prodigal.

Can you relate? If the prodigal's still in the "affair fog" at this time, then one thing is certain: he'll make all the wrong choices. For the life of me, why would anyone whose house is on fire continue to chase the shadow and leave the substance? This is just mind-boggling, because by the time he realizes what has happened, he will have lost his finances, his family, and his reputation through a bitter divorce.

Reflecting on my experience, my prodigal was so blinded by his paramour that he completely disconnected from our family. In my wildest dreams I never thought a husband could be so cruel to his family just to satisfy the selfish whims of a paramour. He gradually stopped texting or replying to my texts. He sent all my calls to voicemail after having blocked and unblocked me a few thousand times. He forgot to pay bills or pay college tuition until reminded to do so. Things became so much worse when he left to go live on his own. It still baffles me as to how he totally distanced himself from his family as if we never even existed.

For me, however, I chose love over hate. I chose to forgive for an apology I never received. I chose to pray for him instead of building anger and resentment. I chose to stand for my marriage because I know God hates divorce. My advice to betrayed spouses is never to engage with paramours since no good will come of it. It's not worth your time or effort. Choose to pray for them instead. Remember: God "heals the brokenhearted, and binds up their wounds" (Psalm 147:3). Leave vengeance for God, because He will do a better job of it than you ever could.

Prayer: *God Almighty, I pray that You remove the spiritual blinders for paramours to see the errors of their ways. May You sever soul ties, heal childhood wounds, and destroy generational curses in the name of Jesus. God Almighty, surround our prodigal spouses with a hedge of thorns and* *wall them in so that they cannot find the paths that lead them away from us. May they encounter You and come to the end of themselves. Dear Lord, may they love what You love and hate what You hate. What the enemy has planned for evil, Father, turn it around for our own good in the mighty name of Jesus. May sleep and rest escape both prodigal and paramour just as God caused sleep to escape the king in Esther 6:1, until they are freed from their sexual immorality. When Abimelech took Sarah, Abraham's wife, You sent him a message he could not ignore. Father God, send them messages they cannot ignore in Jesus's name. Amen!*

Other paramour tactics might include threatening to tell you (the betrayed spouse) about their illicit affair if the prodigal tries breaking things off with the paramour. So keep that in mind when you begin receiving unsolicited calls from strange numbers or getting emails from unknown sources. This threat keeps your prodigal on a small leash since the paramour monitors everything they do. Some go to such great lengths to ensure that a prodigal does not go back to their spouse. However, the smart ones beat them at their own game and confess everything to their betrayed spouses before the paramours do.

The poignant thing that paramours fail to understand is that a prodigal who has cheated on their spouse would most likely cheat on the paramour too. My flesh crawls when I hear that some paramours actually fall for the prodigals. How can you allow yourself to fall in love with another woman's husband or another man's wife? What do you think will come of it but pain, misery, and devastation all around? Do you think you've earned the right to be happy with someone else's spouse? How delusional can you really be? Stop giving yourselves lame excuses to justify your actions.

A real man or woman will never break another man or woman's home to make their own home. End the affair and end it now before it goes any further—that is, if you still have any shred of decency left in you. You need to apologize to the betrayed spouse and simply walk away. This is the least you can do for all the wrongs you have done. Don't think for a second that you deserve any medals for doing what is right, and don't be in a hurry to settle for something that isn't yours to begin with. Think of the innocent children who didn't ask to be included in this drama. You can palpate the pain and hurt they feel. I pray that you choose to do the right thing, relent from your evil ways, and give your life to God. Doing this just might save your soul from the pit of hell, for that's where it's currently headed.

Lessons for Paramours

Stop, look, and listen! Stop putting yourself down, thinking you can only be someone's dirty little secret. You deserve better than that even if you don't think that now or think that you're not good for much else. No one should ever become someone else's second option when it comes to matters of the heart. Know this—God will never give you someone else's husband or wife. Quite trying to seduce them. It only devalues your worth as a man or woman.

Why would you pressure a married person to leave their spouse for you? Why would you even *want* to be with someone capable of inflicting that kind of pain on another human being? Don't be so shortsighted—think long term. If you manage to get the person away from their family and they marry you, what happens when that same pattern repeats itself—but this time with another man or woman? Would you be able to live with the consequences? Adulterous affairs lead only to heartbreak in the long run. The sooner you get that through your head, the better the outcome will be for you. Be patient and wait for the right partner God has ordained for you. You'll find that partner, or they'll find you at the right time. Remember that the wages of sin is death.

Here are some warnings in the Bible about adultery and adulterers:

- "Let marriage be held in honor among all, and let the marriage bed be undefiled; for God will judge the immoral and adulterous" (Hebrews 13:4).
- "You shall not commit adultery" (Exodus 20:14).
- "He who commits adultery has no sense; he who does it destroys himself" (Proverbs 6:32).
- "But I say to you that every one who divorces his wife, except on the ground of unchastity, makes her an adulteress; and whoever marries a divorced woman commits adultery" (Matthew 5:32).
- "If a man is found lying with the wife of another man, both of them shall die, the man who lay with the woman,

and the woman; so you shall purge the evil from Israel" (Deuteronomy 22:22).

- "But I say to you that everyone who looks at a woman lustfully has already committed adultery with her in his heart" (Matthew 5:28).

- "Shun immorality. Every other sin which a man commits is outside the body; but the immoral man sins against his own body" (1 Corinthians 6:18).

- "The commandment is a lamp and the teaching a light, and the reproofs of discipline are the way of life, to preserve you from the evil woman, from the smooth tongue of the adventuress. Do not desire her beauty in your heart, and do not let her capture you with her eyelashes; for a harlot may be hired for a loaf of bread, but an adulteress stalks a man's very life. Can a man carry fire in his bosom and his clothes not be burned? Or can one walk upon hot coals and his feet not be scorched? So is he who goes in to his neighbor's wife; none who touches her will go unpunished" (Proverbs 6:23–29).

- "Every one who divorces his wife and marries another commits adultery, and he who marries a woman divorced from her husband commits adultery" (Luke 16:18).

Other Bible verses on adultery

- "I have seen your abominations, your adulteries and neighings, your lewd harlotries, on the hills in the field. Woe to you, O Jerusalem! How long will it be before you are made clean?" (Jeremiah 13:27).

- "If we confess our sins, he is faithful and just, and will forgive our sins and cleanse us from all unrighteousness" (1 John 1:9).

- "Thus a married woman is bound by law to her husband as long as he lives; but if her husband dies she is discharged from the law concerning the husband. Accordingly, she will be called an adulteress if she lives with another man while her husband is alive. But if her husband dies she is free from that law, and if she marries another man she is not an adulteress" (Romans 7:2–3).

- "This is the will of God, your sanctification: that you abstain from unchastity; that each one of you know how to take a wife for himself in holiness and honor, not in the passion of lust like heathen who do not know God" (1 Thessalonians 4:3–5).

- "What comes out of a man is what defiles a man. For from within, out of the heart of man, come evil thoughts, fornication, theft, murder, adultery, coveting, wickedness, deceit, licentiousness, envy, slander, pride, foolishness. All these evil things come from within, and they defile a man" (Mark 7:20–23).

I have this belief that a person must answer for what they've done in this life, be it good, bad, or evil. Always, always strive hard to do good. Amen! Have you ever noticed in life that it is much easier to do bad than to do good? Nevertheless, I still encourage you to choose to do good instead. Jesus Himself said in Matthew 5:9, "Blessed are the peacemakers, for they shall be called sons of God." I leave you with these words from Proverbs 31:30: "Charm is deceptive, and beauty is vain, but a woman who fears the Lord is to be praised."

Paramours must be honest and answer these hard-core questions about themselves truthfully.

- Does my childhood traumatic event still cause me pain when I think about it?
- Why am I drawn to people who are married?
- Am I really satisfied with being someone's dirty little secret?
- Did estrangement from my ex cause me to devalue myself?
- Do I think I deserve better in a relationship?
- How does my behavior affect my family?
- What will freedom from my childhood trauma look like?
- What will freedom from poor relationship decisions look like?

Four

Betrayed Spouses

A betrayed spouse is a married man or woman who has been betrayed by a spouse through the acts of adultery. As a betrayed spouse, sometimes you have to pay for someone else's sin. That does not mean that your prodigal's sin is your sin but rather that you become a sacrificial lamb for their sins. Unconditional love is amazing because it overlooks what was, tolerates what is, and looks forward to what will be. This is not to say that you condone or tolerate sin but that through your love a sinner might be called to repentance.

The Bible tells us in 1 Peter 4:8, "Above all hold unfailing your love for one another, since love covers a multitude of sins." When your spouse betrays your trust through adultery, the bond between you two is broken—but not beyond repair. Satan wants to destroy the family of God. He knows that where two or three are gathered in God's name, God is there with them. So he takes captive one spouse to separate them from the "herd." That way, he is better able to control them and make his captives do his bidding.

As a grieving and betrayed spouse, you must be prepared to walk the walk of shame for your prodigal, love them unconditionally, and recognize that your unfaithful spouse is not your enemy—Satan is. Loving your prodigal is to live exposed. This action personifies love to a whole other level when you lay down your life for a friend. Remember what Jesus Christ did on the cross of Calvary. You must continue praying for your prodigal until they're released from Satan's clutches.

In the likelihood that your marriage does not survive adultery and ends in divorce, you should know that some betrayed spouses become guarded to protect themselves. It becomes a survival instinct from the deep scars inflicted upon them. Those who dare to venture into another relationship post-divorce may end up bleeding on those who never cut them. If you are a betrayed spouse and decide to retreat into a cocoon and *not* date, I can't say I blame you. Who in their right minds would want to go through this heartache again? However, if you focus on protecting your heart, you can certainly avoid a lot of heartache, but you would end up living only half a life. Love is still beautiful; love is still an amazing and wonderful thing. It feels good to love and be loved in return.

I'll say this to the prodigal spouses and to their paramours: The law of "karma" is coming for you, because guess what—you reap what you sow. Ephesians 6:12 tells us, "We are not contending against flesh and blood, but against the principalities, against the powers, against the world rulers of this present darkness, against the spiritual hosts of wickedness in the heavenly places." If these words don't give you pause, I don't know what would.

Betrayed Spouses as Standers

For the purposes of this book, a "stander" is a man or woman who remains committed to their marriage despite betrayal from a spouse through the acts of adultery. Standing for your marriage is a faith walk and not for the fainthearted. When standing, you encounter God in ways that words alone cannot describe. Your relationship and faith in God grow and deepen as you allow Him to mold, fill, and use your broken pieces to guide and direct your steps. There will be days where you doubt your stand and wish you had never even started—especially those days where you don't see any movements in the physical. Friends and family will call you crazy, a doormat, or simply refer to your situation as pitiful. There will be days where loneliness cripples your stand to a grinding halt. You'd cry a river until your tear glands run dry; and you cannot utter another word of prayer. It is in these moments that you must stand still and know that God is God. He hears the groanings of your heart and will never allow any suffering to be wasted.

While standing for your marriage, you'll lose and gain weight in rapid succession. Don't fret—it happens to the best of us. You'll also experience all kinds of emotions. Sometimes you experience them slowly, one at a time, and at other times they come cascading so fast that you don't know what to do with them. Listen—you're not crazy, only going through emotions you've maybe never dealt with much before. Your body responds by trying to prepare you for fight or flight as adrenalin courses through your veins. When that happens, you need to increase time with God in prayer so you don't despair or become despondent. Get closer to God, for He is your only source of consolation. Desist from focusing solely on your mounting problems, which does you no good. Rather, fix your eyes on Jesus, for His yoke is easy and His burden light. I know this is easier said than done. But I have been down this road before and I'm familiar with the sufferings involved. I still go through these emotions every now and then. Just remember that there's no set time limit to overcome them. They last only for a season; they too shall pass.

Betrayed spouses should know that prayers are like flowers: they take time to bloom. Be patient. One day you'll look back and wonder how the walls of Jericho fell down flat. Then you'll remember and give that bright beautiful smile that can only come from knowing Jesus. He broke through those dark clouds and gave you beauty for ashes. He restored the years the locusts took and gave you a double portion of blessings for every trouble. In Luke 1:45 Elizabeth said, "And blessed is she who believed that there would be a fulfillment of what was spoken to her from the Lord." Jesus is the answer, so look no further than Him.

Your vulnerabilities during your season as a stander increases exponentially, so be careful who you befriend. It is wise to befriend people of same sex as you. Doing otherwise may jeopardize your stand. Remember that the Bible admonishes us to beware of the devil, for he is prowling around like a roaring lion looking for someone to devour. If you leave a crack, he'll slither in and upend your stand. The Bible tells us in Ecclesiastes 4:9–10, "Two are better than one, because they have a good return for their toil. For if they fall, one would lift up his fellow; but woe to him who is alone when he falls and has not another to lift him up." Therefore, join other devout standers in your ministry or find others who understand what you're going through. You need the support you can get from all the right places. A stander must learn to incorporate fasting with prayer, because it helps to edify your spirit as this is spiritual warfare. For me, when things get rough I turn on a Christian radio station and worship the Lord. That always makes me feel better. Standers, dance and sing your heart out until you forget all your reasons to be sad. Dance when the circumstances drown the music out. God's got you, for your name is inscribed in the palm of His hand. He will never forget you, for He knows you by name. God's promises in Isaiah 61:7 should fill you right up: "Instead of your shame you shall have a double portion, instead of dishonor you shall rejoice in your lot."

Remember to take care of not only yourself but also your children if you have any. They are suffering too and are dealing with the situation in their own way. Sometimes we're so blinded by our own pain that we forget theirs. Exercise and eat healthy. Don't gorge on cookies and ice cream alone. Your mind needs to be sharp and alert to make informed decisions. Know that Jesus is the name above every other name, for there's power in the name of Jesus. Seek Him where He may be found. Call upon Him in the day of trouble and He will deliver you. Our God walks upon the water, He speaks to the sea, and makes rivers in the desert. He makes a way where there seems to be no way. Jesus Christ will stand in the fire beside you, for He carries your healing in His hands. There is nothing that our God cannot do, so sing for joy when your heart is heavy.

Remember that God allowed this season for a reason—to draw you closer to Himself. Take courage, standers! This is a season of divine reversal and divine providence. God has called you to stand in the gap for your prodigal spouse's soul and will give you the crown of life in the end. Stick with Him. May the fragrance of favor be upon you in your stand. Just keep praying and hoping, and don't you worry. What good does worry really do but increase your anxiety levels? Matthew 6:34 reminds us that today already has enough problems of its own, so let tomorrow take care of itself. Almighty God will balance the scales in your favor. You need only fix your eyes on the prize. Remember that our God moves in duality—your feet will do the running and the dancing. His mouth will do the speaking in your favor in Jesus's name. Amen!

Standing for your marriage as earlier stated is not a walk in the park. It's not something that comes with a manual. Rather, it's something you learn to do as you go through that experience. Every day throughout your stand you must put on the full armor of God and be ready for battle.

Here's the real kicker, however—have you noticed that the more you pray and fast, often the worse your situation becomes? Can you relate? It can be so frustrating that some standers at this point give up their stand. My advice—don't do it. Your miracle is just around the bend. When you are too weary or just can't walk, simply stretch out your hand and hold on to the hem of Jesus's garment. He'll see you through this ordeal. He has done that before and will do it again. Remember that we are more than conquerors through Christ, who gives us strength. God loves you and will never leave you or forsake you. Rest in that promise and then adjust your crown. I am a stander. "Even though I walk through the valley of the shadow of death, I fear no evil; for thou art with me; thy rod and thy staff, they comfort me" (Psalm 23:4). Read this verse out loud and be refreshed. Joseph said in Genesis 50:20, "As for you, you meant evil against me; but God meant it for good, to bring it about that many people should be kept alive, as they are today."

While standing for my marriage, my anxiety, palpitations, and panic attacks progressively worsened. I experienced all kinds of symptoms, from recurrent headaches to heartaches, tummy aches, and mood swings. I felt loneliness as I had never felt before in my entire life. My mind became a battlefield and kept me awake at night. Some days I cried from the time I got out of bed to when I went back to bed, only to stay completely awake throughout the night. I muttered to myself that this was no way to live but felt very powerless to do anything about it.

Then it happened! I finally figured it out: It is only Jesus who can and will fill this emptiness inside. He can and will make you whole again if only you let Him. We must fix our eyes on Jesus and not on our present circumstances. I know deep down in my heart that this season too shall pass. Since that realization, my situation has drastically improved.

Betrayed Spouses with Prodigals in Multiple Affairs

For the betrayed spouse whose prodigal is involved in multiple affairs, I'd say that you have a bigger fish to fry. I hope you have a larger pan handy. May God help you in your predicament. If betrayed spouses whose prodigals are involved with one paramour are already self-combusting, then imagine those with multiple paramours. Ten thousand fire trucks cannot douse the flames you feel burning deep inside. Talk about a woman scorned! Proverbs 21:9 wisely says, "It is better to live in a desert land than with a contentious and fretful woman." The King James Version translates this verse as "It is better to dwell in the wilderness, than with a contentious and an angry woman." You do not want to be within thirty miles of her. Can anyone really blame her? You brought this on yourself, Mr. Prodigal, if your betrayed spouse finally loses it and goes full-on ninja on you. Even the Teenage Mutant Ninja Turtles are no match for her fury—so don't bother hiring them.

Betrayed spouses in this category should better run and not walk to God. There's nothing that our God cannot do. Let Him be your shield and protection and provide the strength you need to win this fight. Satan often uses your plight to play mind games on you while the battle rages on. My advice? Shut it down as soon as the intrusive thoughts set in. Rebuke the devil and say out loud, "We destroy arguments and every proud obstacle to the knowledge of God, and take every thought captive to obey Christ" (2 Corinthians 10:5). Take courage, "for the battle is the Lord's" (1 Samuel 17:47). Ephesians 6:17 encourages us, "Take the helmet of salvation, and the sword of the spirit, which is the word of God." Use it to defeat Satan and his enemies. God's Word is "sharper than any two-edged sword" (Hebrews 4:12). Don't you ever forget that. When you believe in Jesus Christ, you have the power to call on His name, for there's power in the name of Jesus. John 1:12 reminds us of that power: "To all who received him, who believed in his name, he gave power to become children of God."

Risks of Unfaithfulness to Betrayed Spouses

For betrayed spouses whose prodigals have multiple sexual partners, I sympathize with what you're going through and dealing with. Do they not care how many sexually transmitted diseases are out there? Do they not know that they could catch one and inadvertently expose you to it? How is that fair to the betrayed spouse? I know! I get it! I feel your pain as someone who is walking in your very shoes.

For the life of me, I just don't understand why anyone would jeopardize losing their entire family for a quick lay in the hay with a bottom feeder. Yes! That accurately describes it. Then again, prodigal spouses have no taste. They downgrade from eating on valuable China to eating on disposable paper plates. This temporary insanity could perhaps be traced back to their childhood trauma or negative life experiences. The question is—What happened to them in the past that causes them to act this way in adulthood?

As stated before, this by no means give prodigals a free pass to "Promiscuity Island." Neither does it negate the hell they've put their families through. It just makes sense to find out the root cause of this problem and then take steps toward healing that traumatic life event. Keep in mind that prodigals are wandering lost souls seeking others to fulfill them. Unfortunately, they are looking to fill that need in all the wrong places. No human can take the place of God. Saint Augustine wrote, "You have made us for Yourself, O Lord, and our heart is restless until it rests in You."

Many resources are available for handling sex addiction issues. Find the ones that relate to your case and digest as much information as you can to make informed decisions. Get the help you need sooner rather than later. The Bible tells us in 1 Corinthians 6:19–20, "Do you not know that your body is a temple of the Holy Spirit within you, which you have from God? You are not your own; you were bought with a price. So glorify God in your body." We have to be watchful as Christians and be ready, for there are enemies everywhere. They just change their appearances (evil takes on many faces). This is not just me activating my antenna and sounding the alarm but encouraging you to stand on guard at all times.

What Betrayed Spouses Deserve from Their Prodigals

- Betrayed spouses deserve to be loved by their husbands or wives. The Bible commands husbands to love their wives as Christ loves the church and gave Himself up for her.
- They deserve complete and honest communication from their spouse.
- They deserve to be included in future plans about family and not left isolated like an outsider.
- They deserve to be respected.
- They deserve total commitment and nothing in between.
- Betrayed spouses' children deserve to be loved and cared for by both parents.
- Betrayed spouses' children deserve a full-time and not a part-time father or mother.
- They deserve a spouse who honors their wedding vows, a leader with integrity, one with a moral compass to know that adultery is bad.
- They deserve a spouse who is willing to admit wrongdoing, acknowledge mistakes, and is willing to work hard to make amends.
- They deserve a spouse who asks for forgiveness from God and the family they have hurt.
- They deserve loyalty from their spouse and not betrayal.

- They deserve a spouse who is not a serial cheater or repeat offender.
- They deserve a spouse who is willing to get help, agrees to marriage counseling, and is prepared to get with the program in its entirety.
- They deserve a husband or wife who does not resort to stonewalling, deflection, resentment, anger, hatred, gaslighting, and manipulation to get their way.
- They deserve a spouse who even if they fall, are willing to get back up and do what is right before God and man.
- They deserve a spouse who puts family first and makes time for family.
- They deserve a spouse who is brave enough to admit wrongdoing regardless of the consequences and doesn't scurry off like a coward for weeks, months, or years on end without communication.
- They deserve a spouse they can be proud of and want their children to emulate.
- They deserve a husband or wife who engages in communal activities within the church and the community to make this world a better place.
- They deserve partners who do not constantly put themselves in compromising situations and are wary of the type of company they keep.
- They deserve a spouse who has no business setting up dating profiles online.

- They deserve a spouse who chooses them and their families first, the first time.
- They deserve a spouse who chooses godly friendships and refuses to keep bad company.
- They deserve spouses who honor their wedding vows and uphold the sanctity of marriage.
- They deserve to have the best spouse in the world, and their children deserve to have the world's best mom and dad.
- They deserve spouses who put God first in everything and draw their family closer to God.
- They deserve a spouse who stands up for what is right by cutting off all contact with the paramour at discovery.
- They deserve spouses who know when they have crossed the line, confesses their sins, and are willing to do better.
- They deserve spouses who do not live double lives, do not get stressed out by who they've become, and do not pile all the blame on their spouses.
- They deserve a spouse who loves them for them.

How Your Prodigal's Behavior Affects You and Your Marriage

Do you know what it feels like to be told by your spouse that they don't love you anymore, that they've never been in love with you and should never have married you? Do you know what it feels like to be told by your spouse that you have no value and have not added any value to their lives? Have you any idea what it feels like to be told by your spouse that you've grown apart, don't get along, and that somehow it's entirely all your fault? Do you know what it feels like to be told by your spouse that they love you but aren't *in* love with you?

If you're married to a prodigal spouse, I have a pretty good idea that you know exactly what I'm talking about. Their behavior leads you to a place you'd rather not go. The patience and boundaries of your love and grace are stretched so thin and bruised in ways that challenges the foundations of your faith as a Christian. Have you ever dealt with a broken heart? It never beats the same once broken. Betrayed spouses often feel so isolated and alone when their prodigal walks. All communications cease and the betrayed spouse is mostly now treated as an outsider.

The points above are not exhaustive. Prodigals say these things with a straight face, without emotion as if that's normal—but it's not. When this happens, they are usually spoiling for a fight to give them a reason to continue in their fit of rage. Don't engage them, because if you do it will backfire on you. I know from experience and also know it's not easy to stay quiet when they come at you like a bulldozer. I have gone Mike Tyson on my prodigal many times and delivered quite a few knockout punches myself (metaphorically speaking) off course. My advice? Don't do it. Your home is not a battlefield and nothing good will come of it. Think of the children if you have any. They are watching, listening, and learning useful life lessons from you, be they good or bad. This is no time to look for old boxing gloves but rather to put on the full armor of God. Nailed it? Oh, no! For some of us, we still let out a few choice words before our boiling blood cools down. And don't even get me started with the "zip your lips" thing. That's not even in my vocabulary at the moment. If you've never encountered a prodigal spouse's behavior, then you're probably not the wisest sage in the clouds right now. Until you've been in someone else's shoes, you can't tell that person how to tie their own shoelaces. So don't go offering unsolicited advice as if you know it all. Believe me—you don't.

Though every situation is different, betrayed spouses still go through fire and water with their prodigals. In my humble opinion, I think the prodigal spouse gravitates from one polar opposite to the other, neither being less painful than the other. It is a complete and total nightmare. If children are involved, they, too, may suffer anxiety and depressive symptoms, headaches, tummy aches, and mood swings. I can't possibly name them all here. Their grades at school may take a hit or they may act out in unusual ways. Keep them grounded and pray for them. Never keep them away from your prodigal if they want to maintain a relationship with them unless if protecting them from apparent danger. Get them the mental health support they need at the earliest possible time. Unfortunately, we cannot choose our own families.

I know as a betrayed spouse you'd probably wander around like a zombie in your pajamas for the first few weeks following D-Day (day of discovery). Never mind—we all did that. It's nothing to be ashamed of. I need you to feel what you feel but then you must get up and tend to your kids. They need you to show some strength as the only stable parent they'll probably have for a long time. Get help from family and close friends if you need to, but be careful who you air your family dirty laundry to as this could come back later to haunt you. Please don't go it alone, however. Invite Jesus into your mess and let Him grow new gardens from dead graves. Amen! The Bible tells us in 1 Peter 4:12–19 about suffering as a Christian:

Beloved, do not be surprised at the fiery ordeal which comes upon you to prove you, as though something strange were happening to you. But rejoice in so far as you share Christ's sufferings, that you may also rejoice and be glad when his glory is revealed. If you are reproached for the name of Christ, you are blessed, because the spirit of glory and of God rests upon you. But let none of you suffer as a murderer, or a thief, or a wrongdoer, or a mischief-maker; yet if one suffers as a Christian, let him not be ashamed, but under that name let him glorify God. For the time has come for judgment to begin with the household of God; and if it begins with us, what will be the end of those who do not obey the gospel of God? And "If the righteous man is scarcely saved, where will the impious and sinner appear?" Therefore let those who suffer according to God's will do right and entrust their souls to a faithful Creator.

Grief and Physiological Symptoms Experienced by Betrayed Spouses

For the betrayed spouses left behind or abandoned, their self-esteem is totally wiped out. In order to survive, they must go into survival mode. At first they isolate and cut off from the world. They experience grief and go through the grieving process. It's like grieving a deceased spouse.

I experienced something very similar. I was very emotional at the beginning, barely able to get out of bed. I ate very little because I had no appetite and lost thirty-five pounds rather quickly. Wow! Trauma made me look "hot." Not funny at all. I can afford to crack jokes now, but back then I felt like a caged animal seething with anger. As I said earlier, I went from not eating anything at all to consuming any and everything I could find. I could eat an elephant and a whale for breakfast with room left over for a hippo. Other times I skipped both breakfast and lunch and prayed that I could swallow a morsel for dinner. Can anyone relate? Yes! It was that bad for me. From there my anxiety levels peaked. This eventually culminated in frequent panic attacks, heartburn and headaches. Since I experienced these on a regular basis, I had to go on antianxiety medications to help me cope with activities of daily living. It was indeed a very dark and miserable time for me. Some days I cried so hard that my whole body shook from sobbing. The interesting thing here was that my grief strengthened my relationship with God at a much deeper level. It helped me understand that God was always with me and loved me unconditionally. I just failed to recognize that in my pain.

I discovered that on certain days my anger just turned into sadness. I moped around all day and had no interest in anything—one of the classical signs of depression, I guess. I never felt like discussing my problems with anyone except for one of my besties who had also gone through a similar experience.

Most days I poured out my heart to God. I prayed, fasted, did novena after novena, and then prayed some more. I simply kept busy to stop the raging battle in my mind. Some days were better than others off course. But during those awful days my anxiety and panic attacks were like something out of a horror movie. I would curl up on the couch with my hands wrapped across my upper torso to stop my heart from beating out of my chest. I thought I was going to die from the palpitations. At night, panic attacks took over and made falling asleep a living nightmare. When the attacks came on, I would jump out of bed, grab my rosary, and pop my antianxiety medications into my mouth, mumbling the name of Jesus for help. I felt dizzy with a sense of dread, as if something bad were going to happen. I hated that sinking feeling. As I paced the room the whole time this was happening, I contemplated going to my daughter's room to awaken her. I just needed another human being by my side so I didn't feel so all alone. But as soon as I got to her room, I always stopped myself. I didn't want to burden her with my problems. She was already dealing with the situation the best she could. I simply turned around and walked back to my room with tears streaming down my face. As the tears flowed freely, I cupped my mouth to muffle the sound that could alert her to my distress.

Most days I would remember my holy water and oil sitting on my nightstand and grabbed those to anoint myself. My thoughts then were that just in case I didn't make it through the night, I would have at least given myself the last rites as a Catholic Christian. What a way to go! With rosary in hand, I would silently pray for God to help me and make these panic attacks stop. I found that praying my rosary and the chaplet of divine mercy helped a lot during these attacks. It so happened that every time I recited the rosary, the attacks would quietly stop much as they had began. It at least took my mind off things for the time being. At the end of my prayers I mostly climbed back into bed holding unto my husband's long-sleeve shirt until I fell asleep out of sheer exhaustion. It was my mind's way of having my prodigal close to me since he wasn't physically there, and his shirt still smelled of him. This daily ritual became part of my new normal.

One time the attack was so bad that I almost called 911. I had to notify my primary care provider, who then ordered an EKG and recommended that I wear a Zio patch to monitor my heart rhythm for two weeks. I did as ordered and thank God—the results did not indicate any major pathological findings.

One time during my panic attacks, I called out to my husband, but it soon dawned on me that he wasn't there, that he was gone and no longer living with us. That realization made the attack unbearable that night. Just as with all the others, that attack passed, and this, too, would pass in the name of Jesus. Amen!

My emotions swung from one end of the spectrum to the other. Some days it felt as if I were a volcano about to erupt. To be quite honest, my emotions were all over the place much like a roller-coaster. I struggled with accepting my current situation for a long, long time until I finally did. Sometimes I experienced my emotions all at once. It was all so very frightening. Thank goodness—I'm at a better place now and have come to accept my present situation.

When not working, I like to listen to gospel music, do my journal entries, or simply watch movies on Netflix. I also frequent marriage blogs and prayer walls and watch YouTube videos featuring marriage restoration testimonials. I've also read a lot of self-help books to educate myself about issues on adultery. The pandemic of 2019–2021 hasn't made it very easy to socialize or do much else. However, with each passing day my confidence in God has grown leaps and bounds, and I know I'm going to be okay with or without my prodigal spouse.

Every once in a while I experience setbacks as palpitations and panic attacks rear their ugly heads. But they are much more manageable now and are no longer severe, as they were at the very beginning. I'm learning to take one day at a time and have recently incorporated exercise into my daily routine. In life we cannot always change our circumstances, but we can change our attitude. As they say, "You can't change the weather, but you can grab an umbrella."

One thing I have learned from going through this experience is that whatever life throws at you, whether they're problems that are as big as planets, life-altering crises, or normal bumps and blips, you must humble yourself and surrender it all to God. You must never seek to micromanage your situation or go it alone. Turn it over to Jesus, who is more than willing to lend a helping hand. Believe me—it makes all the difference. Sometimes you have to experience the bad to appreciate the good, and sometimes the heart needs to be broken for the soul to heal. Proverbs 11:29 assures us that "He who troubles his household will inherit wind, and the fool will be servant to the wise."

The most heartbreaking thing I experienced during the lowest point in my life was when I actually contemplated suicide. I researched ways to end my life very quietly without alerting anyone. I was so broken, and in that moment I saw no escape. The pain I felt crushed my very soul and I wanted it all to end. For me, then, that was the only way out. Even now my hands shake as I think about that experience. While writing these words, I get emotional as things may very well have turned out differently for me. I have prayed and asked God for forgiveness and believe He has forgiven me too. Can you imagine what that could have done to our precious daughter? Thank You, God. Thank You for showing me that there was a better way out of this. You showed up when I needed You the most and pulled me out from the pit of despair. You loved me when I couldn't even love myself. You made Your voice louder and drowned out the other voices in my head. You told me I was precious in Your sight so much so that Your only begotten Son, Jesus Christ, died for me. Your unconditional love pieced through my darkened soul and made beautiful flowers bloom once again from lonely tombs. How can I repay the Lord for His goodness to me? My soul sings praises to my God for all He has done for me.

Never give up, my beautiful and brave betrayed spouses. Help is on the way. Hold on! Corrie Ten Boom, a Dutch Christian watchmaker, wrote, "I've experienced His presence in the deepest darkest hell that men can create. . . . I have tested the promises of the Bible, and believe me, you can count on them." Amen!

When negative thoughts come to your mind, rebuke them and confide in a friend. You must seek help and know that your life is worth saving. God loves you no matter what your prodigal says or may have voiced concerning you in the past. Don't believe those lies. The only report about you that is true is the report of the Lord. For His report says that you are free, that you are healed. His report says *victory. Hallelujah!*

Another problem that betrayed spouses face is changes to their living dynamics in the home once the prodigal leaves. The abandoned spouse may be left to shoulder the financial responsibilities of running a home and are left to care for the children alone, who also experience pain and grief. This new living situation is particularly hard on them. Never forget the fact that we tend to neglect our kids when wallowing in our own pain. Betrayed spouses need counseling, and I remember those days when I goggled the Internet like a crazy lunatic until my fingers were numb. I just wanted to understand what was going on and find support from others who were going through the same thing or have had similar experiences like mine.

Going through these experiences could be very humbling for the betrayed spouse. Remember—marriages just don't deteriorate overnight. The process happens gradually over the years. People grow apart, stop communicating, and take each other for granted. Couples stop putting God first due to the craziness of life and it is a costly mistake people often make. We must know that no one can ultimately fulfil us—only God can. As humans, it is okay for us to be "perfectly imperfect." We should stop giving other people so much power over us, for we can only complement each other at best.

God must always come first in our lives, and communication is key. Through this channel we can resolve issues before they start. Remember that "a stitch in time saves nine." Couples must have a plan regarding what to do when marriage storms hit and carry out that proposed plan to quickly repair any damage. No couple is given a marriage journal or a blueprint that contains step-by-step guidelines on how to deal with marital crises when they occur. Couples may consider having a marriage survival kit handy or a crisis plan (fail-safe mode) to deploy during emergencies. All families need one.

Be accountable for your mistakes, take ownership for your actions, and make amends. Don't run away and separate from your family when trouble hits. Only weak men and women do that. This choice further erodes trust between you and your spouse. Remember your wedding vows. Marriage is sacred and should be treated as such. When you need help and support, get it now, not later, because "procrastination is the thief of time." My father (God rest his soul) always said, "Time and tide wait for no man."

If one spouse is vulnerable to affairs, have accountability partners to help and support them. There is no shame in asking for help. Don't let pride ruin the plan God has for you. There is a reason you both tied the knot. Recognize that family members are not disposable. They are not objects to be used and then discarded when you think that they are no longer of service to you. These are individuals just like you with feelings. Don't give up on them without a fight. Love them now while you can because one day God will ask for them back. "The battle is Mine," says the Lord, so give it to God in prayer. If you love your spouse, you will learn to forgive them no matter what. We should learn to love one another because God first loved us. Love bears all things and does not keep record of wrongs. "Love covers a multitude of sins" (1 Peter 4:8). That does not in any way signify that we should become doormats or fools for love. We as couples should set boundaries as forms of checks and balances, helping to protect those involved. Always apologize when you've wronged your spouse or child.

Our children are watching and learning from us every day and will model and bring into their marriages what they've learned from us. We must not only teach but also show our kids how to live godly lives through words and actions. The Bible says, "Train up a child in the way he should go, and when he is old he will not depart from it" (Proverbs 22:6). We as parents can do this with God's help. It is never too late to make things right. Keep in mind that the grass is not always greener on the other side. It is greener where you water it. Further, always read your Bible if you are a Christian. It was written for a purpose and contains words that will help you and your family live godly lives.

Triggers: What Are They?

Triggers are described as "reminders associated with your partner's sexual acting out and emotional abuse, or other relational abusive behaviors" (Blythe, n.d.). These reminders can cause a person to feel overwhelmingly sad, anxious, or panic-stricken. For betrayed spouses, until you've completely come to grips with your spouse's betrayal, you'll have triggers, flashbacks, and intrusive thoughts. Really! This almost sounds like post-traumatic stress disorder to me. As a betrayed spouse, you should identify your triggers and make a plan regarding how to deal with them when they occur. You might think of journaling, joining a support group, and seeking professional help if needed.

When a husband or wife has triggers, the unfaithful spouse should show extra love and remorse despite the harsh words and anger that may be coming from the betrayed spouse. This is for those who still have their spouses with them and are working toward reconciliation. It's a time for both spouses to immerse themselves in the ocean of God's love through His Word.

I don't know what I would have done if God had not become my anchor and shield during this difficult season. If you're alone, try not to self-isolate except in times spent in your prayer closet. Ensure that you have a support system—a community of Christian folks who may have experienced the betrayal of a spouse and have come out on the other side. Educate yourself and be prepared to go through periods of crescendo and diminuendo with your emotions. It's like riding a roller-coaster. You know how it goes if you've ever been on one. Could you imagine falling into an icy lake at subzero temperatures? You get rescued, only to be thrown into a fiery lake of burning sulfur before you've had time to adjust. Yes! That sounds about right when dealing with a double-minded prodigal.

Triggers are like salt added to injury, especially when the perpetrator is MIA (missing in action). You have to pray to develop "armadillo skin" to stop yourself from punching holes through all your walls. When triggered, try to stay in control, because this feeling is just triggering your rejection switch. Redirect your thoughts at once. Hold them captive and make them obedient to Jesus Christ.

Things That Bring On Triggers in Betrayed Spouses

- Seeing your spouse's name pop up somewhere
- Texts, call, emails
- Social media
- Couples holding hands
- Smelling their cologne in public places
- Movies and music
- Games
- Restaurants
- Church

- Work
- Seeing transport or swift trucks with Bible verses written on them
- Books
- Kids and pets

Did we miss anything? Let us know what your triggers are and how you have dealt with them or are still dealing with them when they occur. Go to our YouTube Channel, "Hope for the Betrayed" (tiny. cc/ctotnz), to share your experiences with triggers.

Five

Observations and Suggestions for Dealing with Prodigal Spouses

Healing from Betrayal

Let's be clear: sorrow is not sin and neither is righteous anger. Gratitude does not cancel out grief in any way. You must allow yourself to feel what you feel as a betrayed spouse. Let no one tell you how to feel it or when to stop feeling it. It takes time, and people heal at their own paces. "Blessed are those who mourn, for they shall be comforted" (Mathew 5:4). "Rejoice with those who rejoice, weep with those who weep" (Romans 12:15). Wow! The Bible is truly a blueprint for how to handle life situations.

Betrayed spouses go through the grieving process because they're mourning the loss of a marriage and the loss of a spouse. Healing takes time. You may be strong one day and can stand on your own two feet, but the very next day those same feet turn to jelly and buckle under you. The heart-wrenching pain that comes along is probably something you've never felt previously. I don't think you can adequately describe the pain of betrayal. Somedays I cried so hard that my entire body shook from all the pain I was feeling, which was so thick you could almost cut it with a knife.

I bet my cries could have made God want to put on earmuffs. I prayed for Him to come down quickly to my aid and heal my broken heart. At times the yearning for a simple touch or a shoulder to cry on became so overwhelming that I simply hugged my curtains, placed my head on my walls, or collapsed into my pillows for comfort. I just needed to be held, as we all do sometimes. It's in moments like these that you begin to appreciate the need for human touch and companionship. Humans were not created to be alone, especially husband and wife—they are one flesh. As Genesis 2:18 states, "Then the Lord God said, 'It is not good that the man should be alone; I will make him a helper fit for him.'"

Prodigals may never fully grasp the carnage they leave behind when they reject and abandon their spouses and families and walk away. It is pure selfishness and a complete lack of human decency. This behavior portrays just how evil humans can be. It does not reflect the love of God; neither does it uphold the vows you made on your wedding day. Jesus Christ broke barriers by teaching us to extend that love even to our enemies. Say what, now? Listen—in order for you to be a true follower of Christ, you must take up your cross and follow Him. Though, my situation seemed insurmountable, I just could not give up on my prodigal, having been taught by my parents early on never to give up on God or family. These words I have kept close to my heart, and they have guided me to this day.

My question is this: How does a husband and father walk away from his wife and children in pursuit of happiness? How does a wife and mother walk away from her husband and children? I can understand if the relationship was abusive and the woman or man leaves for safety reasons, as they should. No one should be placed in a position to be in fear for their lives ever, especially in a family setting. I'm pretty sure this is not what God designed marriage to be. Other than that, I may never fully understand the forces at play when prodigal spouses break their commitments and leave. That curiosity made me dig deeper into uncovering the mystery behind their sudden decisions to leave.

From what I garnered, it holds true that the devil is out to destroy families. It makes it easier for him that way, to spread the seed of discord among God's people. It's almost like killing two birds with one stone when he annihilates one member of a family. Those left behind will be devastated and scattered, ultimately leading to separation and divorce. Nevertheless, we can defeat the devil and beat him at his own game through the power of prayer. There is power in the name of Jesus and we as Christians are assured of this through the resurrection power. Through Jesus's name we can rise from the pit of despair, gird up our loins, and be ready for battle. We must learn to fix our eyes on Jesus at all times regardless of the circumstances. Our victory in battle is assured when we align ourselves with Christ. Spiritual warfare can be won only by using spiritual tools, so I strongly suggest that you put on the full armor of God. Remember what the Bible says in Ephesians 6:12: "For we are not contending against flesh and blood, but against the principalities, against the powers, against the world rulers of this present darkness, against the spiritual hosts of wickedness in the heavenly places." This is a scary thought, but the same Bible equally tells us in 1 John 4:4, "Little children, you are of God, and have overcome them; for he who is in you is greater than he who is in the world." Amen! Further, we have the power to choose between good and evil. The Bible encourages us to choose good always. So bear this in mind before you go full-on ninja or kung fu panda with your prodigal.

There is so much more involved in a single-family unit. Once formed, it extends far beyond just husband, wife, and children. Whatever experiences we acquire, both good, bad, and ugly, spill over to the next generation. Our marriage scars tell our story. Because of this, it is ever so important to walk your talk and pray to break generational curses. Annihilate evil with the power of the Holy Spirit before they take root and become part of your family legacy. As a child of God, you must position yourself to hear from God and discern the truth by the power of the Holy Spirit. Every day you must decide to take up your cross and follow Christ. The Bible tells us in James 5:15, "The prayer of faith will save the sick man, and the Lord will raise him up; and if he has committed sins, he will be forgiven." Amen!

Emotional trauma can take a lifetime to heal. Consider this before you trade your children's welfare for temporary pleasures. It is not worth it in the long run. When healing from the traumas of betrayal, remember that there is no rush, as I have said many times before. Take your time to heal properly. You don't get a medal for getting over yours first. You must be allowed to heal at your own pace and take one day at a time. When you get to your destination, wait for others to catch on. My hat's off to those who have gone through this life-changing experience and have come out on the other side. Though they bear deep scars, they still choose to do good.

For betrayed spouses on the road to recovery, you may think that you've finally turned a corner, only for these waves of emotions to creep up on you out of nowhere. You crumble once again and slowly begin the steep climb back up. I want you to know that it's okay. It's not uncommon for that to happen. Remember that the pain you feel waxes and wanes. It comes with the territory—just don't go it alone. No person is an island. Take God with you every step of the way. Learn to lay your burdens down at the feet of Jesus and take the break you so richly deserve. Rest when you need it. Though your problems may be big as planets, they'll turn to pebbles when He speaks. Amen! Affirm this truth that the battle is the Lord's and the Lord's alone.

Prayer: *I pray that God will give you justice. I declare and decree John 14:14 that if you ask anything in His name, you will be heard and helped, Amen! May God give you strength to never give up and miss your blessing. Remember the persistent widow in the Bible (Luke 18:1–8). God gave her justice in the end, and I prophesy that same ending for you in the name of Jesus. Amen!*

Please remember to get the help you need through counseling, group support, education, your chaplain or pastor, friends, family, health care providers, and so on. Do what works for you. We all need fewer repeat offenders in our marriages, especially when we've been betrayed by those we love. Remember also that wayward spouses tend to pile up collateral damage like a tornado through a traffic jam. That's why it is ever so important to put on the full armor of God. This allows us to fight this spiritual battle with victory in mind. Did any of these groups help you in your journey toward affair recovery? Please let us know by commenting on our YouTube channel (tiny.cc/ctotnz).

Prayers for Your Prodigal Spouse

Dear Lord, please give our spouses a new heart and a new spirit. Remove their hearts of stone and give them hearts of flesh (Ezekiel 36:26). Improve lines of communication and grant them godly sorrow that lead to true repentance of their sins (2 Corinthians 7:10). I pray, God Almighty, that you remove spiritual blinders for them to see the errors of their ways. I stand on Luke 4:18, in which Jesus quoted the words of Isaiah: "'The Spirit of the Lord is upon me, because he has anointed me to preach good news to the poor. He has sent me to proclaim release to the captives and recovering of sight to the blind, to set at liberty those who are oppressed.'" Father God, Isaiah 35:5 says, "Then the eyes of the blind shall be opened, and the ears of the deaf unstopped." Please release our spouses from the shackles of the enemy and set them free in Jesus's name. Amen!

Jesus, I decree and declare Ephesians 5:8 over our prodigals: "For once you were darkness, but now you are light in the Lord; walk as children of light." Amen! I stand on the word of God in Acts 26:18, which says, "To open their eyes, that they may turn from darkness to light and from the power of Satan to God, that they may receive forgiveness of sins and a place among those who are sanctified by faith in me." Amen! Father God, cover our prodigals with a hedge of thorns and wall them in as seen in Hosea 2:6–7 so that they cannot find the path that lead them away from us and our families. Psalm 119:18 says, "Open my eyes, that I may behold wondrous things out of your law." Father God, grant our spouses the willingness to seek Your truth, for the truth shall set them free. Amen!

Lord Jesus, make our marriages a living metaphor of the beautiful relationship You desire to have with Your church (Ephesians 5:25). Lord, You know how much we're hurting right now. You know how much we love and miss our spouses and want our family back together. But, God, we're heartbroken and scared that our non-communication might cause them to forget us. We pray that this separation will quickly come to an end and for marriage restoration to take place. Father God, help us to trust Your will for our marriages, and if the outcome isn't as we hoped, we pray that Your will is done. Lord, we now lay our prodigals at Your feet for You to do with them as You please. Amen!

Food for Thought

As a married man or woman, focus on creating a safe place for your spouse to unwind. Be a safe haven where they can be vulnerable and tell their little secrets without fear of judgement or criticism. As betrayed spouses, we can learn to be more skillful in the way we communicate with our spouses so they do not misconstrue the message we are trying to convey. We can begin by saying something like this: "I understand you're skeptical about becoming vulnerable around me because of the giant wall between us. I'm going to work on my weaknesses so that you can eventually feel safe with me. I'll try to keep uncovering the part I played in creating such an unsafe place for you. I won't rest on my laurels until you feel comfortable enough to open up to me."

Sometimes when we hit rock bottom we ask the wrong people for help. Beware the kind of people you unload your dirty laundry secrets to. Some of them do not have good intentions toward you and would love to see you fail. Even if the situation seems dire, you must remember that there's nothing our God cannot do.

Philemon 1:12–13, 15, 22 says, "I am sending him back to you, sending my very heart. I would have been glad to keep him with me. . . . Perhaps this is why he was parted from you for a while, that you might have him back forever. . . . At the same time, prepare a guest room for me, for I am hoping through your prayers to be granted to you." Amen!

We should also keep in mind that not everything that's broken is meant to be fixed. In such situations, we cannot be certain of what the future holds. But I do know that it's best to ward off desperation and maintain a positive attitude. Sometimes life throws us curve balls, giving us perhaps not what we had hoped for or what should have been. Do not let pride stall your recovery process. Wayne Dryer said, "You can either be a host to God or a hostage to your ego. It's your call." He went on to say that people should "have a mind that is open to everything and attached to nothing." That way you limit the likelihood of offending someone because of the sensitive world we live in. I couldn't agree more. My dear betrayed spouses, Sarah Young writes,

> If you encounter a problem with no immediate solution, your response to that situation will take you one way or the other. You can flip and lash out at the problem, resenting it and showing how weak you are. On one hand if you chose this option, know that that would quickly drag you down to a place you'd rather not be in. On the other hand, you can use the problem to propel you to see your life from another angle. The choice is yours. From that vantage point, you can view the obstacle that frustrated you as only a small speck of dust in the sand.

With God on your side, these problems you perceived as big as tall mountains will turn to pebbles when He speaks! Turn toward your maker and see the light of His presence shine on you. Though it is true that the pain and brokenness caused by adultery is devastating and can shake the foundations of your faith, don't allow one painful experience to color your whole future. A broken heart can be healed by God. Once adultery happens, it cannot be undone. Since there's no way of putting toothpaste back into the tube, we must learn to roll with the punches and forge ahead wherever the road leads.

The unfaithful spouses' identities will forever be tied to whatever they give their hearts to. Prodigals are in the habit of deflecting and delaying the inevitable once the truth comes out. There's no need for that, because the sooner you begin the process of discovery, the sooner you can begin working toward reconciliation. According to Abraham Lincoln, "You cannot evade the responsibilities of tomorrow by delaying them today." I would say this—man up and take the bull by the horns. That's the least you can do for trading your billion dollars for only a quarter.

For betrayed spouses who are serious about winning their spouses back, you must lay your burdens at the feet of Jesus and love them unconditionally. Love is the key. Love is the only way, and love will show them the way back home. 1 Peter 4:8 says," Above all hold unfailing your love for one another, since love covers a multitude of sins." Do not resort to hating your spouse either. I know most of us struggle with this. Proverbs 10:12 tells us, "Hatred stirs up strife, but love covers all offenses."

I know a lot has been placed onto your shoulders as a betrayed spouse. But James 1:12 states, "Blessed is the man who endures trial, for when he has stood the test he will receive the crown of life which God has promised to those who love him." You must learn to forgive those who have hurt you. It's not easy and may take a while to get there. You forgive not because the person who hurt you deserves it but for your own peace of mind and healing. This is not to say that you must play the role of doormat. No! Use wisdom. "Behold, I send you out as sheep in the midst of wolves; so be wise as serpents and innocent as doves" (Matthew 10:16).

Have it at the back of your mind that some prodigals never immediately apologize for what they have done. Doing so would make them admit wrongdoing. So they avoid doing that at all costs. Do not be perturbed. The burden of carrying that guilt and shame will eventually run its course. They'll come to the end of themselves and hopefully do the right thing. Read the story of the prodigal son in the Bible (Luke 15:11–32). That should encourage you and give you hope for the future.

Prayer: *Father God, bless all betrayed spouses and keep them from straying from Your truth. Grant them courage to help bring prodigals who are wandering back to You through prayer. Strengthen them, Lord, and remove all obstacles that hinder marriage restoration. Grant them the spirit of forgiveness and love. Make them love hard when it is hard to love. Help them to forgive their spouses as they have been forgiven. Remove the paramours from their spouses' lives and cause sleep and rest to escape them until they return to You and to the families they left behind, I pray in Jesus's name. Father God, I pray that my own prodigal will love what God loves and hate what God hates (Psalm 97:10–12). I pray that he will encounter God and come to the end of himself. I stand on Mark 10:9, which says, "What therefore God has joined together, let no man put asunder"; and Isaiah 54:17, which tells us, "No weapon that is fashioned against you shall proper." Lord*

Jesus, every tongue that rises up against us must fall. Amen! Dear Lord, protect my marriage from all who seek to destroy it. I pray that You separate an ungodly and unscriptural relationship from ever taking root in this union, in Jesus's name. Root out any form of adultery, lustfulness, pornography, lies, deceit, pride, and secrets from our lives in Jesus's name. Amen! Make us quick to recognize and turn from sin and cleanse us from all unrighteousness. Help us to uphold our wedding vows and respect the sanctity of marriage. Father God, never let us jeopardize the whole relationship in favor of a non-working part in Jesus's name. May we look to You, O God, to heal and make us whole again. Amen!

Remember that since all have sinned and fall short of the glory of God (Romans 3:23), we should endeavor to extend grace to our lost spouses since we have also received extraordinary grace from God.

Question: If your prodigal returns home after many years in the wilderness, would you take them back? Let us know on our YouTube channel (tiny.cc/ctotnz).

According to Rick Warren, "It is always more rewarding to resolve a conflict than to dissolve a relationship." I agree with him. You don't want to become included in the statistic of failed marriages, because the devil topples 50 percent of married couples into the murky waters of divorce (American Psychology Association, 2021).

My dearest betrayed spouses in Christ, know that God loves you no matter how your situation turns out. Even though you did not break your marriage commitment, you still carry the burden of shame and guilt from your betrayal. I want you to rise up and keep your heads held high because you are sons and daughters of the king. Rise up, therefore, and adjust your crown. Let us not become too eager to see the product and miss out on the crafting and refining of that product. Patience is a virtue, so allow God to work on your prodigal while you wait. There are many blessings, too, in the waiting. You just have to keep your eyes open to find them. God is building you up for His kingdom. Jeremiah 16:21 says, "Therefore behold, I will make them know, this once I will make them know my power and my might, and they shall know that my name is the Lord."

May your Christ-centered character be what makes you most beautiful as you continue to pray and fast for your prodigal's return to Christ. May you be a fragrance of life and the sweet aroma of Christ among prodigals being saved.

Prayer: *Lord, I trust You without reservation no matter what happens. You have a purpose and a plan in my unique situation. Amen!*

Your Prodigal Spouse's Lack of Good Judgment

Some prodigal spouses' strange rationale for refusal to get help following discovery is the fact that they don't want to "spoil their good name"—that is, the facade that prodigals project outside for others to see versus who they really are. They somehow believe that they are too damaged and so must work harder to please others in order to be loved. They continue struggling to keep the lid on from revealing who they really are.

The fear is that when people find out this truth about them, they'll face rejection and no one would love them. These are some of the lies they've told themselves for so long that they become part of who they are. Society has not made it any easier, particularly for men who are placed on a pedestal and taught to behave or act in a certain way as providers and leaders right from childhood. The expectation and pressure to measure up and be perfect takes its toll.

Some others believe that stopping their addiction would only benefit their betrayed spouses. Does that make any sense? That analogy certainly didn't make sense to me. It only goes to show just how lost these prodigals really are. There are other categories of prodigals who smoke, drink alcohol, or take drugs, while some others are addicted to sex. The thing is, these are unhealthy avenues they are choosing to travel. Over-indulging in any one of these to such degree that it impedes a person's senses of reasoning, causing them to act irresponsibly or behave in unacceptable ways, signals a need to address the issue. By the way, you should not be engaging in extramarital affairs as a married man or woman. As awful as this might sound, do you know that some prodigals actually think they deserve a medal for not indulging in all the other behaviors? I mean, where do these male prodigals get off thinking that they're God's gift to womankind? How would you respond to some of these assertions?

You don't get first prize for not smoking, drinking, or taking drugs over adultery. Doing one does not cancel out the other. Neither has a great outcome when done excessively. I can feel my blood boiling as I write these words. I mean, how dare you tell betrayed spouses not to cough up water from the last time you tried to drown them? One is not better than the other. I know all humans are flawed, but give me a break! Prodigal spouses know that adultery is bad. In fact, most put themselves in harm's way because they go looking for an "escape." They want to be free of life's pressures. Tough luck! I guess you shouldn't have decided to get married when you knew you were grossly ill-prepared for married life. A real man or woman faces their problems head on. They don't shrink back or retreat indefinitely. So put on your big-boy pants and get cracking to win this race.

Married men or women ought to be weary of the kind of company they keep. They have no business creating profiles on dating apps. What did they think would happen putting themselves out there? You're already taken. Invest in your relationship and quit looking for an outlet for fun. It never ceases to amaze me when I find middle-aged men dressed up like teenagers in ripped jeans, riding loud motorbikes while wearing giant sunglasses, or driving swanky convertibles. If you've chosen to regress to your younger selves to boost your ego, then be prepared to take the heat that comes along with it. Why complain about being disrespected by your spouses? I'm pretty sure your poor spouses who are obviously still in shock from your weird transformations, are trying hard to differentiate the husband from the son. You made your bed, so you either lie in it as it is or grow up already—because your spouses are not your parents. When you know you are addicted to something, admit that you have a problem and that you need help. That is the first step that actually shows signs of maturity in a grown adult male or female. Then appreciate the support provided for by your loved ones. It makes you so attractive when you take full responsibility for your actions. Problems arise when you deny the obvious and look for someone else to blame for your shortcomings.

The sad thing here is that many betrayed spouses at this point become free-floating guilt magnets as they take on blame for their spouses' failings and make up lame excuses for their behaviors. Listen! It's not your fault that your spouse is acting out and refusing to grow up. You can do only so much. Pray and support your prodigals as much as they'll allow. Then go look for help in all the right places. Don't forget that you, too, need help from all the stresses piled up on you. Look around—you don't have superpowers or a flying cape tied around your neck. You're no Superman or Wonder Woman, so quit trying to fly!

Let's digress a bit here. I think it's awesome that young couples are required to go through premarital classes before marriage. The importance of this cannot be overemphasized. The question here is this: Are these classes comprehensive enough for married life? I think married young couples should *continue* to be mentored by elders of the church. The interests in successful marriages should not end with premarital classes alone. Don't you agree? There also should be an interest in the kind of lives these young married men and women lead since they are the leaders of tomorrow.

I don't particularly agree with the adage "You can't teach an old dog new tricks." You see, as humans we learn something new every day. Our ministers and church leaders have a major role to play here. There should be ministries for married couples, for those revolving around resolving marital conflict, and some others offering support for the separated and divorced. These last groups are often the ones mostly forgotten, and it's quite shameful. I just feel that church leaders could do more by serving as accountability partners for members of their Christian communities. If these measures were securely in place, I think a lot of marriage hiccups we see today within the first three, five, or seven years might have better chances of survival. Problems could be caught early on and addressed before spiraling out of control and beyond repair.

Another disappointing fact is that some ministers or pastors are not even in the business of trying to bring the lost sheep back into the fold. When betrayed spouses alert leaders of the church about their marital woes, they are too often met with nonchalant attitudes from church leaders who are reluctant to do the work involved in salvaging broken marriages or healing marital discord. They give up even before trying. In fact, they are often the first to tell you to abandon ship. They imply that the best way to go would be making a clean break through divorce or an annulment and then starting over. It's sad to watch how easy it is for them to give up on marriages without so much as lifting a finger. I cannot fathom that this is happening within a community of God's people. Where have we gone wrong? What can we do to fix these issues as Christians? The Bible clearly lays out steps to follow in dealing with sin in the church. Jesus said in Mathew 18:15–17,

> "If your brother sins against you, go and tell him his fault, between you and him alone. If he listens to you, you have gained your brother. But if he does not listen, take one or two others along with you, that every word may be confirmed by the evidence of two or three witnesses. If he refuses to listen to them, tell it to the church; and if he refuses to listen even to the church, let him be to you as a Gentile and a tax collector."

Standing for Your Marriage

As stated earlier, standing for your marriage is not a walk in the park. It's not something that comes with a manual. Rather, it's something you learn to do as you go through that experience. Every day throughout your stand you must put on the full armor of God and be ready for battle. We are more than conquerors through Christ who gives us strength. Remember that only Jesus can and will fill the emptiness inside. Your walk with Jesus certainly began with baby steps. These things take time. Slowly but surely you can turn the corner and start feeling better. That glimmer of hope that was once lost can be reignited once more within your soul. We must fix our eyes on Jesus and not on our present circumstances.

This might sound repetitive, but it is much needed to soothe a heart that's hurting. Ever wish this had never happened to begin with? I don't know about you, but the very man who broke my heart also makes it skip a beat. It may sound crazy or a little bit cliché, but just as Selena Gomez said in her album, "The heart wants what it wants." After all these years and considering what he's put our family through, my husband still makes my heart pitter-patter. There—I said it! You can judge me all you want.

One thing that bothers me is when a woman standing for her marriage is told to be consistent and patient with her betrayer. They say not to let him see your anger when he visits; smile at him and welcome him with open arms. You can even flirt with him— after all, he is your husband. Prepare his favorite meals during such visits and avoid bringing up any marriage issues. Don't stalk him on social media either.

Give me a second here while I go scream into my mailbox. I'm not the one who broke the commitment, in case you've forgotten. He left because he "wasn't happy" according to him and we both were disconnected emotionally. Well, tough luck, big guy. I wasn't happy either, but that did *not* give me the right to go looking for happiness outside of marriage. I understand. I get it. Your frustrations are valid. But what good does it do if we keep going around in circles like a merry-go-round? Someone has to be an adult in this mess.

Just know that if you want to save your marriage, you have to fight the right battles using the right tools. Your spouse is not your enemy—Satan is. It will take your prodigal time to trust your changes to ensure that it's permanent and he feels safe enough to return. I know that the betrayed spouse wasn't any less vulnerable to affairs than the prodigal, but we must bury the hatchet and focus on what's really important. Galatians 6:9 encourages us, "Let us not grow weary in well-doing, for in due season we shall reap, if we do not lose heart."

Betrayed spouses must be honest and answer these hard-core questions about themselves truthfully:

- Does my childhood traumatic event still cause me pain when I think about it?
- Why do I crave validation from my betrayer?
- In what way does my spouse's affair affect me?
- How does my spouse's addiction affect our family?
- Do I take all the blame for our marital woes?
- Has my spouse shown any signs of remorse for their affair?
- Why do I want to remain in this marriage following betrayal?
- What will freedom from my traumatic event look like?
- What will freedom from my spouse's addiction look like?

Six

Finding Grace in Marriage Storms

According to Joseph R. Cooke, "Grace is the face that love wears when it meets imperfection." Rejection hurts, especially when coming from a loved one. You might be tempted to reject them right back or write them off as a lost cause.

But wait! Don't be in a hurry to toss your loved one out as someone too damaged for Jesus, even if they're involved in multiple affairs. In Luke 5:32 Jesus said, "I have not come to call the righteous, but sinners to repentance." There's still hope for tough cases like your prodigal's. Your prayer every day should be "Blood of Jesus, wipe away all handwriting of hatred and rejection from my life in Jesus's name. Amen!" Post this in strategic places around your home where you can see it and affirm this truth. Have faith! For there's no heart too hard for God to heal, no pain too great for God to ease, and no marriage too damaged that cannot be restored. Amen! Isaiah 60:22 says, "I am the Lord; in its time I will hasten it." If there's one thing you must remember, remember this:

"Your Maker is your husband, The Lord of hosts is his name; and the Holy One of Israel is your Redeemer, the God of the whole earth he is called. For the Lord has called you like a wife forsaken and grieved in spirit, like a wife of youth when she is cast off, says your God." (Isaiah 54:5–6)

Jeremiah 32:27 says, "I am the Lord, the God of all flesh; is anything too hard for me?" You must remember that the path to joy is often through self-denial while the part to misery is often through self-indulgence. You may be rolling your eyes and must have forgotten that I can't really see what you're doing. Look! I know it's unfortunate when your circumstances don't line up with God's promises. This is where doubt creeps in and you begin wavering in your faith. Guess who's there to egg you on. That's right—the devil, because he is the father of all lies. Resist him and be like David in Psalm 57:7—"My heart is steadfast, O God, my heart is steadfast! I will sing and make melody!"

For betrayed spouses I would say this: hang in there for just a little while longer, especially if your life's not in danger from abuse or violence. Jesus has you in the palm of His hand and hasn't forgotten about you. This can seem implausible especially for long-standers. But I still encourage you to hold on to this truth. There's nothing more righteous than defending those who cannot defend themselves. You fit perfectly into this category and Jesus Christ is in the business of doing good. He'll make a way and give you peace once again. Remember the words of 2 Corinthians 12:9: "'My grace is sufficient for you, for my power is made perfect in weakness.' I will all the more gladly boast of my weaknesses, that the power of Christ may rest upon me." Don't always view your circumstances as a tomb but rather see them as a womb—a kind of rebirth in which things old shall become new.

I know this is a scary time for you and your family because of fear of the unknown. I get it! "The anticipation of death is worse than death itself." Even so, I want you to believe that there is purpose in every season, especially for those that don't make sense. The problem with us these days is that we've lost the act of waiting as Christian disciples. You don't know what God is protecting you from by allowing this season in your life. I want you to know that patience is a weapon that forces deceit to reveal itself.

So don't go looking for a temporary fix. It will only leave you feeling emptier inside. Remember: God will not hold us accountable for how our spouses treat us but *will* hold us accountable for how we love our spouses in spite of their dispositions. Romans 5:8 reminds us of God's love for us: "God shows his love for us in that while we were yet sinners Christ died for us."

Prayer: *Lord, I am praying for all prodigals who have gone astray. Lord, You know where they are in the pigpen of life. They are wandering and away from their spouses and loved ones in the far country. Lord, I pray that You remove spiritual blinders for them to see the error of their ways and turn them from darkness to light. Lord, I decree and declare that You release them from the power of Satan through Your grace, that they may receive forgiveness for their sins and a place among those who are sanctified by faith in You. I pray that You go right now and bring home our spouses and all the other wandering lost souls to the glory of Your holy name. Amen!*

Keys to Marriage Restoration

Patience, empathy, humility, and compassion are fundamental to marriage restoration. The Bible says in Romans 8:28, "We know that in everything God works for good with those who love him, who are called according to his purpose." Remember, too, that miracles come in all shapes and sizes and are unique to our individual situations. There's no one-size-fits-all. Sometimes we may not see it, feel it, or hear it, but God is always working regardless.

On a prayer wall from Rejoice Marriage Ministries was written the following: "The greatest handicap is fear. The best day is today. The most useless asset is pride. The dumbest mistake is giving up. The best gift is forgiveness. The most unfailing love is God's love for you." I think this writer might be on to something here. Like many others, I certainly do not want to give up. But sometimes it gets too lonely and too overwhelming. During these times I find myself asking God, "When does it all end?" Can you relate?

Regi Campbell said, "Your marriage is up to you. It will become what you make of it. You are responsible. You are the leader. Love isn't a hole you fall into; it's a choice you make." Do you agree with her analogy? Does it make sense to you at all? I know it takes two to make marriage work, and unfortunately only one to destroy it. I have also read that people need to be restored before they can be led. What if restoration does not occur? Does this mean that such people cannot be led and are therefore lost forever? I don't have all the answers, but what I do know is that there is a reason for everything. If one door closes, another window is open some-where. You just have to find it through the eyes of faith.

Don't give up. Hold on to hope that God will make a way. He made a path through the Red Sea, He sent manna from heaven—and He won't fail you. Think about Job from the Bible. Could you imagine what he endured? He held unto his faith, knowing that God gives and God takes away. I indulge you to do the same and wait on God. Remember: you can't microwave maturity or micro-wave God. I know it's not always easy, for "Uneasy lies the head that wears the crown." I get it! But you must also remember that in the position you're in, no amount of manipulation, begging, kick-ing, and screaming will work—but God.

Not too long ago a very wise man told me that sometimes in life you have to lose everything to find everything. Better yet, Jesus asked in Mark 8:36, "For what does it profit a man, to gain the whole world and forfeit his life?"

In my situation with my prodigal, I tried extending grace to him despite the mounting problems I was facing. But the more I prayed, the more dire my situation became. Why do you think that is? The devil is a liar, and he will stop at nothing to make your situation look as if prayer isn't working when in fact it is. Humans tend to focus only on the physical (things they can see). Don't let your tunnel vision deter you from getting to your promised land. God is always working whether you believe it or not, and His Word will not come back void but will carry out the purpose for which it was sent. Amen!

I often wonder why prodigals are so stubborn. I soon learned that if our sole purpose of wanting our prodigals back is to replace the loneliness we feel with their presence, then we've simply missed the mark. Only God can fill us up. Giving another person that kind of power will always leave us disappointed and empty inside. It's simply a void they cannot feel.

Additionally, restoration is so much more than getting back together with our spouses. It's a spiritual battle for the salvation of our spouse's soul. Marriage restoration is about winning souls for Christ and if He has called us to stand and handed us this torch, rest assured that He has also equipped us for the battle up ahead. The victory in the end will always be for His glory because God will never share His glory with anyone.

In regard to prodigals, I have come to the conclusion that pride and instability must have something to do with their double-mindedness. The Bible says in James 1:8, "That person must not suppose that a double-minded man, unstable in all his ways, will receive anything from the Lord." For those of us going through betrayal from adultery, Rick Reynolds from Affairrecovery posits,

"Healed individuals who have recovered from betrayal can tremendously help those currently going through this experience because experience is the best teacher. Betrayed spouses should connect with others in their community so individuals are not left to go through this alone. Also, in order to enhance the likelihood of success in affair recovery, unconditional dignity and respect must be essential elements included in that process."

This is true since both wayward and betrayed spouses' self-worth has plummeted to ground zero and could have been part of what led to the affair in the first place. The pain caused by adultery can be healed, but only if people are willing to do the work needed for healing to take place.

Here are some of the things I did to keep my sanity and self-respect during the worst time of my life. These include but are not limited to the following:

- Prayer and fasting—as a Catholic, I prayed as if my life depended on it and incorporated novenas into my routine. I also booked mass for my family on a regular basis and lit candles for us on the altar.
- I read a lot of self-help books to understand what's going on in the mind of a prodigal spouse.
- I watched highly educational videos to help me make informed decisions in areas peculiar to my situation.
- I regularly visited marriage blogs and ministries and participated in online discussions to gain a new perspective on marital issues of interest.
- I journaled to help me see my progress—or regression as the case may be—and took the steps required to forge ahead.

- Sometimes I reached out to my prodigal via text or email during special occasions or holiday celebrations. Don't take it personally if they reject your kind gesture. Most times they will. Just don't flood them—use wisdom and guidance from God.

- I sent out online prayer requests to various religious ministries to have intercessory prayer warriors pray for my special intentions.

- I encouraged my prodigal to rededicate himself to God by providing reminders periodically. Be careful, though, as you don't want to appear self-righteous.

- I stopped discussing anything marriage-related with family and friends.

- I tried being myself and not reacting to everything my prodigal said or did. Beware—they will intentionally get on your nerves to see if you've changed.

- I eliminated many aspects of social media stalking. It increases your anxiety and impedes your road to recovery, especially when you become exposed to things you cannot handle.

- I refocused my attention to doing the things I liked, that brought me happiness, like redecorating, gardening, singing, dancing, and writing. Find your niche and start something today.

- I made time for my family. Yes, kids need our attention too. Don't forget your pets if you have any furry friends lying around. They need your love too.

Jesus said in Matthew 17:20, "Truly, I say to you, if you have faith as a grain of mustard seed, you will say to this mountain, 'Move from hence to there,'" and it will move; and nothing will be impossible to you." Remember what Franklin Roosevelt said during the Great Depression: "The only thing we have to fear is fear itself." Let's take our rightful place and stare down the devil with the power of the living God. "For God did not give us a spirit of timidity but a spirit of power and love and self-control" (2 Timothy 1:7).

Before you react to any provocation, take a deep, long, cleansing breath and count to three. Then speak as the Holy Spirit leads. Amen! Remember that Satan is the author of immorality and he knows the flavor of sin to bait his hook with. Those who fall for his lies become his captives and do his bidding. Remember also that God has given us power in the name of Jesus Christ to resist the devil and he'll flee from us.

Again I say: listen! Your prodigal is not your enemy—Satan is. Though he would like to convince you otherwise, don't fall for it. Aim your arrows and shoot at the real culprit. He's no cupid. Whatever you do, don't flirt with this fallen angel or he'll thrash you about like wheat. Second Timothy 1:12 reads, "Therefore I suffer as I do. But I am not ashamed, for I know whom I have believed, and I am sure that he is able to guard until that Day what has been entrusted to me."

Seven

What Could Go Wrong?

There is so much hype about wedding vows these days. Could it be that wedding vows are now so "yesterday" or simply overrated? In case you're wondering, the answer is an emphatic no! You couldn't be farther from the truth. Marriage is still sacred, and the wedding vows made between a man and woman on their wedding day are still a covenant that just cannot be broken. Their union is eternal—period.

Call me crazy or old-fashioned if you must, and then proceed to read Mark 10:9: "What therefore God has joined together, let not man put asunder." I am in agreement with this statement, and spouses who dissolve their marriages on a whim or for frivolous reasons ("irreconcilable differences") must answer to God for their disobedience. God hates divorce. It's really that simple. Malachi 2:16 says, "For I hate divorce, says the Lord the God of Israel, and covering one's garment with violence, says the Lord of hosts. So take heed to yourselves and do not be faithless."

You cannot but agree with me that the divorce process is treacherous at best. It brings out the worst in people. The lives of those who have gone through divorce are forever changed. Don't take my word for it. Maybe a trial will convince you. But I wouldn't do that if I were you.

When marriage crises arise down the line, one is never short of good advice from well-meaning family, friends, and colleagues. Everyone becomes an expert and has something to say about your marriage. Some people may advise you to give your prodigal space since they requested it. They tell you not to push your prodigal or you'll further alienate them from you. True. Others may tell you to leave your prodigal in God's capable hands, for He has not given up on them and will continue to pursue and bring back your prodigal to Himself. So very true!

However, God will never interfere with your prodigal's free will. People have the freedom to choose good or bad. Some others might just tell you that it's time for your prodigal to go, that you deserve better and all that. Maybe that's true or false depending on the situation. I hate these kinds of answers especially on a Q & A. I never quite seem to get them right.

Now back to what we were discussing. Prodigals are wandering, lost souls riddled with guilt, shame, and self-condemnation. I cannot say this enough. They carry a huge burden (wounds) mostly self-inflicted. As family members who care for them and their well-being, it is imperative that we pray for them daily and love them unconditionally.

Again, 1 Peter 4:8 says, "Above all hold unfailing your love for one another, since love covers a multitude of sins." Wow! Love is so amazing, and the number of times *love* is mentioned in the

Bible is outstanding. In the King James Version it's mentioned three hundred ten times—one hundred thirty-one times in the Old Testament and one hundred seventy-nine times in the New Testament. It's mentioned three hundred forty-eight times in the New American Standard Bible, five hundred fifty-one times in the New International Version, and five hundred thirty-eight times in the New Revised Standard Version. Also, note that before Jesus transcended into heaven, He told His apostles this: "A new commandment I give to you, that you love one another; even as I have loved you, that you also love one another" (John 13:34).

First John 4:8 proclaims, "He who does not love does not know God; for God is love." Loving one's prodigal is not a job for the faint of heart. It is a debilitating and an emotionally draining saga, mixed with a bunch of crazy feelings that totally overwhelm you. It is almost like a perpetual holding place (a kind of purgatory) you'd rather not be in as a stander. I don't know how anyone can go through this without God. Betrayed spouses certainly need God to fill them up during this storm so they don't keep running on empty. The Bible tells us in Ecclesiastes 3:1–2, "For everything there is a season, and a time for every matter under heaven: a time to be born, and a time to die; a time to plant, and a time to pluck up what is planted."

In all of this there's always light at the end of the tunnel. My father would always tell me, "Every cloud has a silver lining." Now I understand what he meant all those years ago. I love you, Dad. I know you can hear me. In our moment of grief we must not forget that God makes beautiful things out of messy material. Isaiah 61:3 (RSV) says, "To grant to those who mourn in Zion—to give them a garland instead of ashes, the oil of gladness instead of mourning, the mantle of praise instead of a faint spirit; that they may be called oaks of righteousness, the planting of the Lord, that he may be glorified." I love the following quote about waiting on the Lord from Isaiah 40:31: "They who wait for the Lord shall renew their strength, they shall mount up with wings like eagles, they shall run and not be weary, they shall walk and not faint."

The Bible goes on to say in 1 Peter 3:13–17,

Now who is there to harm you if you are zealous for what is right? But even if you do suffer for righteousness' sake, you will be blessed. Have no fear of them, nor be troubled, but in your hearts reverence Christ as Lord. Always be prepared to make a defense to any one who calls you to account for the hope that is in you, yet do it with gentleness and reverence; and keep your conscience clear, so that, when you are abused, those who revile your good behavior in Christ may be put to shame. For it is better to suffer for doing right, if that should be God's will, than for doing wrong.

Prayer: *I pray that whoever is reading this right now that You, Almighty God, shall fill them up. Heal their brokenness and complete the work You began in their families in Jesus's name. Amen! I pray that You, Father God, restore their broken marriages. Lord, I pray that You* *bring all prodigals back to their senses and remove all obstacles from their paths. Bring them home, Lord Jesus. Father God, make their restored marriages a living metaphor of the beautiful relationship You desire to have with Your church (Ephesians 5:25). May their marriage testimonials draw all people to You and may all who see them long to have that kind of relationship with You in the mighty name of Jesus. Amen and amen!*

Eight

Adultery in Our Modern-Day Society

What on earth are "irreconcilable differences"? I don't recall that being part of the wedding vows. If you're a strong Christian like me, then you'll probably understand why my blood boils every time I hear that "irreconcilable differences" nonsense mentioned in a divorce proceeding. I take wedding vows seriously and view marriage as a sacred union between a man and a woman. Why does adultery not carry any consequences in our divorce courts? Is it that sexual immorality has become so gallantly displayed by unfaithful spouses that we have accepted it as the norm in our society?

Quite frankly, I think the courts should revisit some of the reasons for divorce. Since prodigal spouses want to live a life of no consequences, they should be held accountable for their actions by making them pay huge alimonies to their betrayed spouses. Prodigal spouses who want to shelve their responsibilities, including those who show no remorse for their actions, should not be rewarded for it. It's like giving them a free pass to do more damage to their already hurting families. How do you justify an adulterous spouse getting a get-out-of-jail-free card in a marriage that they so witfully destroyed? This makes me so mad, because unfaithful spouses never seem to pay for their crimes or atone for their sins.

Many betrayed spouses have endured years of physical, emotional, mental, and financial abuse from their partners. They deserve to have the moon, if they asked for it, as a small token for the hell they've been through. I think divorce courts could do more by crafting better justifications for divorce and executing stiffer penalties for adultery. I'm not talking about dangerous situations where the spouse or children's lives are in imminent danger. No! That's not the focus in this book. It is for those categories where unfaithfulness in marriage causes much devastation to families.

Adultery has been painted as exciting by our society and therefore carries no consequences. The Bible, however, tells us differently as there are dire warnings and penalties for those who commit acts of adultery. You cannot put into words the price women and innocent children pay when caught up in the mess of adultery. For these children, parental wounds lead to emotional tombs. And we wonder why there are so many children and adults with mental health disorders in our society. Medical professionals are quick to diagnose and put labels on our children when in fact they should focus on addressing the root cause of their mental health issues. It is when and only when that happens that we might see a decline in the number of cases. There might be a correlation between traumatic childhood experiences and mental health disorders (Harvard Women's Health Watch, 2021; Mock and Arai, 2011).

Our world can overcome the pervasiveness of today's promiscuous lifestyle if we change our ways and turn away from sexual immorality. Yes! It is possible through Jesus Christ. We cannot just be hearers of the Word of God—we must also become doers of His Word. Let us give our younger generations a chance and a reason to want to do better. This we can accomplish by modeling good behavior. We must seek to imprint on our children positive moral codes and values. The Bible tells us in Proverbs 22:6, "Train up a child in the way he should go, and when he is old he will not depart from it." J. R .R. Tolkien in *The Return of the King* wrote, "It is not our part to master all the tides of the world, but to do what is in us for the succor of those years wherein we are set, uprooting the evil in the fields that we know, so that those who live after may have clean earth to till. What weather they shall have is not ours to rule."

Nine

My Take on the Pathogenesis of a Prodigal Spouse

For you who have dealt with a prodigal spouse before or are currently dealing with one, here's my take on their pathogenesis:

Phase 1 of the life of prodigals is characterized by secrets and lies to cover up their actions. They hide their laptops, cell phones, and text messages. They delete texts, call histories, emails, and so on. They sleep with their cell phones tucked underneath them and don't answer their calls when you're present. They go to the bathroom or basement to use their devices. When they are caught in their web of lies, they deny, deflect, and enter the next phase.

Phase 2: the blame game. Here the unfaithful (prodigal) spouses see the betrayed spouses as the root of all evil. They blame their spouses for everything that has gone wrong in their lives and play the victim. They make excuses for coming late to appointments and stay out late from work because they are "working." They have no good explanations for extra charges made on credit cards or financial statements. The betrayed spouses' gut instincts tell them that something is wrong, and it usually is. The prodigals call their spouses "crazy" when they question their behavior, which has so drastically changed. They dress differently and stay well groomed. They go to the gym to look toned and sometimes buy their spouses unexpected gifts for no apparent reason. Note to self: it is usually to ease their guilt and shame for what they are doing or have already done. They often engage in unusual sexual behaviors in the bedroom—something they obviously picked up from their paramours. This gradually progresses into the next phase.

Phase 3: the pendulum swing. At this phase the prodigal is confused and conflicted, vacillating between you and their paramour, not wanting to give either up. One minute the prodigal is nice to you and the next minute their evil twin takes over. You both go at each other's throats a few times before things further escalate, and it's not for the better. Tempers run short and the threats of leaving have been uttered a couple hundred times. If the affair has not been discovered at this point, the prodigal gets into fights with you to give them a reason to leave or you'll be forced to kick them out to quell the craziness in the home. The prodigal likes the idea because it gives them reasons to stay with their paramour. They talk about you and their family life situations with the paramour. The prodigal disparages you to gain their confidence. This slowly progresses to the next phase.

Phase 4: the prodigal goes "no contact." They do not respond to your communication attempts and blocks and unblocks you a few thousand times. If they are an in-home prodigal, you're probably sleeping in separate bedrooms. The prodigal appears and disappears at will and without a care in the world. Electronic devices are glued to their hips, and they care more about their devices than you. Your children are confused and worried that they might be responsible for what is going on. No! They are not, and it's important that you help them understand that. On the order hand, if your prodigal spouse has already separated from you and is now leaving with their paramour, they would tell you that they need "space" to think things through. You may not see or hear from them for days, weeks, or even months on end. Quite frankly, I think it makes things easier for them to continue to see their paramour without having to answer to anyone or take responsibility for their actions. This gradually goes into the next phase.

Phase 5: false starts. When all goes well between you two, the prodigal spouse might make attempts at coming home. If you're a stander by now and have been prayerfully standing for the restoration of your marriage, then you may see a couple of these false starts, especially if communication lines have opened up once again. The prodigal spouse may have very well experienced the fact that the grass isn't always greener on the other side. Who knew? This phase may take anywhere from a couple of months to years. They simply vacillate between their spouse and paramour. The job of the stander is to stay focused on God and let Him deal with your prodigal. If all goes well, then it usually progresses into full-blown restoration. It is now that the faithful stander's stand truly begins. The devil will fight to woo your prodigal spouse back and will not wave the white flag that easily. So be on your guard and pray without ceasing. This phase may also progress to a protracted separation or go through to divorce.

Phase 6: restoration and affair recovery. Once your marriage is fully restored, your prodigal might bring themselves to apologize for what they've put you and your family through. You now begin to see glimpses of the man or woman you first married. They at this point agree to counseling, are receptive to getting support and accountability partners, and gradually becomes indoctrinated into the family life once again—and by this time must have broken off all contact with the paramour. The stander must not rest on their laurels. You must continue to fast and pray for your family and always put God first above everything else. The prodigal might be willing at this stage to confess to you what life was like for them in the far country ("pigpen" life). Getting your prodigal to talk is like pulling teeth. Let them take the lead and just be a good listener. However, your prodigal must also tell the truth and answer all your questions so that "trickle-down" truth does not set your restoration backward and give the devil another foothold. Work with your counselors to do what's best for your individual situations and family. For those who have divorced, restoration and remarriage can still occur if it is the will of God. Proverbs 21:4 says, "Trust in the Lord with all thine heart; and lean not unto thine own understanding" (KJV).

Marriages Plagued by Adultery Can Be Healed

Marriage involves two people who should work together to make it work. Sadly, as noted earlier, it requires only one of them to destroy it. Couples must continue to invest in their relationship. Once they stop, they begin taking each other for granted, and that spells trouble in the long run. Married couples must avoid keeping secrets from each other in order not to give the devil a foothold. Create a safe environment for your spouse to air their grievances and forgive as often as necessary. That way resentments don't build up over the years.

If you need help as a married couple, get it now, not later, so wounds don't fester. You both fell in love and pledged to be there for each other through good times and bad. When marriage crises arise, face them together. Do not leave and abandon your spouse and family in pursuit of happiness. Remember that the grass is not always greener on the other side—it's greener where you water it. Always put God first in all you do and invite Him in when trouble hits.

As a prodigal, how would you feel if you overheard your wife or husband in prayer asking God not to allow your children to marry someone like you? Ponder on it for a second and let that sink in. If you have children, know that you are modeling the type of behavior that is acceptable to them in a family setting. Let us raise up kids we can be proud of and be husbands or wives whom we as parents would want our children to marry. Marriages rocked by adultery can be healed if both spouses do the work required for healing to take place. Be patient with your spouse—healing takes time once one spouse is betrayed. Practice unconditional love with your spouse and you both must learn to respect each other.

Wouldn't it be wonderful if there were a type of machine that measures where things really stand in marriages? That way we know what to do when the arrow on the scale is pointing toward red. For me, I believe marriage should be worked on and nurtured daily and not just during crises. Communicate with your spouse and compliment them daily. Be content with what you have and never stop investing in each other. Revelation 21:4 assures us, "He will wipe away every tear from their eyes, and death shall be no more, neither shall there be mourning nor crying nor pain any more, for the former things have passed away." Amen!

For those of you wondering where I stand today in regard to my own marriage, rest assured that I am still standing for my marriage to be restored in God's perfect timing. I do not need validation from anyone to know that my life is precious in God's sight. I know that I am beautiful, I am valuable, I am a child of God, and my life is worth saving. Because Christ lives, I can face tomorrow. Today I am seeing my life for the very first time through a different lens. Lord, You are my recue story.

As betrayed spouses, we must not let the grief of abandonment, the sting of betrayal, and the pain of rejection color our lives. As Christians we cannot pick and choose the seasons we want in our lives. We must have faith and believe that the same God who saw us through spring and summer will also see us through fall and winter. Though the seasons of life may change, we serve a God who changeth not. He is the same today, tomorrow, and forever. I leave you with this: though your enemies may sit on the throne, you rule them by prayer. Amen!

Resources

Adams, L. (2018, July 16). The truth stands up. Retrieved from http://www.allgoodthings.nyc/new-blog/2018/7/16/the-truth-stands-up

American Psychology Association (2021). Marriage and divorce. Retrieved from https://www.apa.org/topics/divorce-child-custody

Beam, J. (2019). My spouse wants a divorce. What do I do? #1 (YouTube video). https://marriagehelper.com/my-spouse-wants-a-divorce-what-do-i-do/

Blythe, A. (n.d.). When your trauma is triggered. Retrieved from https://www.btr.org/when-your-trauma-is-triggered/

Boom, C.T. (n.d.). Quozio 2021. Retrieved from https://quozio.com/quote/f29b3095/1025/ive-experienced-his-presence-in-the-deepest-darkest-hell

Campbell, R. (2014). What radical husbands do: 12 steps to win and keep your wife's heart. Radical Mentoring Publisher.

Cooke, J. R. (n.d.). Grace is the face that love wears when it meets imperfection. Retrieved from https://quotefancy.com/

quote/13601/Joseph-R-Cooke-Grace-is-the-face-that-love-wears-when-it-meets-imperfection

Einstein, A. (n.d.). Retrieved April 22, 2021, from https://www.brainyquote.com/quotes/albert_einstein_130982

Fray, M. (n.d.). Must be this tall to ride [Blog]. Retrieved from https://mustbethistalltoride.com/an-open-letter-to-shitty-husbands/

Gomez, S. (November 6, 2014). The heart wants what it wants (YouTube video). Retrieved from https://www.youtube.com/watch?v=ij_0p_6qTss

Harvard Women's Health Watch. (2021). Past trauma may haunt your future health. Retrieved from https://www.health.harvard.edu/diseases-and-conditions/past-trauma-may-haunt-your-future-health

Harvey, D., Tripp, P. D., & Gilbert, P. B. (2016). Letting go: Rugged love for wayward souls. Grand Rapids, MI: Zondervan.

Lewis, C. S. (2011). Choices turn the central part of you. Retrieved from https://www.goodreads.com/quotes/7659880-every-time-you-make-a-choice-you-are-turning-the   Lewis,

C. S. (n.d.). True progress. Retrieved from https://tifwe. org/c-s-lewis-on-true-progress/

Lincoln, A. (n.d.). You cannot evade the responsibilities of tomorrow by delaying them today. Retrieved from https://www. brainyquote.com/quotes/abraham_lincoln_10173

Lusko, V. (2015). Through the eyes of a lion. Nashville: W Publishing.

Marriage Revealed Ministries. (n.d.). From broken to blessed. Retrieved from https://marriagerevealedministries.com/

Martin, L. (n.d.). The recognition of sin is the beginning of salvation. Retrieved from https://www.azquotes.com/ quote/1090149

Mock, S. E., and Arai, S. M. (2011). Childhood trauma and chronic illness in adulthood: Mental health and socioeconomic status as explanatory factors and buffers. Retrieved from https://pubmed.ncbi.nlm.nih.gov/21833299/ doi:10.3389/ fpsyg.2010.00246

Newton, I. (July 5, 1687). Philosophiæ Naturalis Principia Mathematica. Publisher: Benjamin Motte.

Rejoice Marriage Ministries (2021). Restoring lives and healing hearts. Retrieved from https://www.rejoiceministries.org/

Roosevelt, F. D. (March 4, 1933). Inaugural address as published in Samuel Rosenman, ed., *The Public Papers of Franklin D. Roosevelt, Volume Two: The Year of Crisis, 1933*. New York: Random House (1938), 11–16.

Reynolds, R. (2007, 2021). Affair recovery. Retrieved from https://www.affairrecovery.com/about-us/ricks-story

Tolkien, J. R. R. (1955). The return of the king. Republished (2003) by Del Rey. Retrieved from https://www.penguinrandomhouse.com/books/179217/the-return-of-the-king-by-jrr-tolkien/9780345339737/

Tony, E. (2019, August 14). Satan's tricks and traps. Tony Evans sermon [YouTube video]. Retrieved from https://www.youtube.com/watch?v=DIqzGP5CudY

Warren, R. (May 15, 2018). How to manage conflict and stay married in ministry. Retrieved from https://pastors.com/how-to-manage-conflict-and-stay-married-in-ministry/

Wright, H. N. (1999). Loving a prodigal: A survival guide for parents of rebellious children. Colorado Springs: Chariot Victor Publishing.

Young, S. (2013). Devotional journal for everyday of the year. Jesus calling: Enjoying peace in His presence. Nashville Tennessee: Thomas Nelson Publishing Inc. ISBN 979-1-5914-5188-4